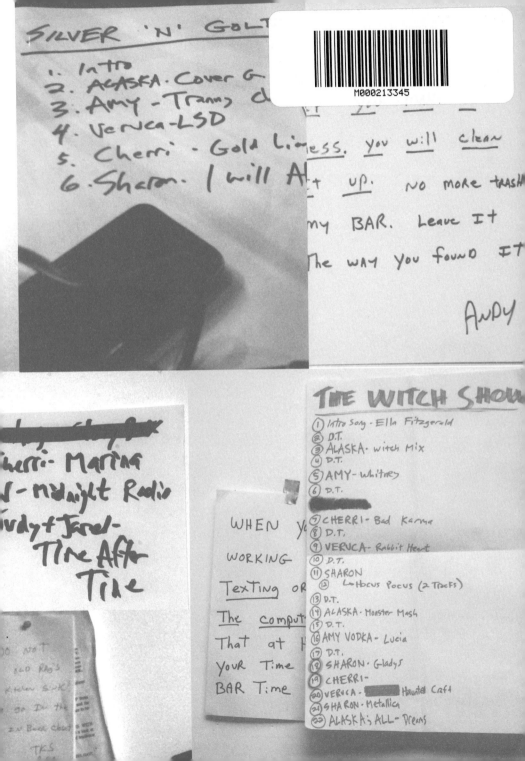

SILVER 'N' GOLT...

1. Intro
2. ALASKA. Cover G...
3. Amy - Tranny d...
4. Veruca-LSD
5. Cherri - Gold Li...ess. you will clean
6. Sharon. I will A...+ uP. NO MORE TRASH

...my BAR. Leave It

The WAY you found IT

ANDY

M000213345

...herri- Marina
...N-midnight Radio
...rdy + Jared-
TIme AFter
TIme

JO NOT
...LO RAG'S
...itchen SiNK
...o IN the
IN Bucc cbout
TKS

WHEN Yo...
WORKING
TeXTING or...
The comput...
That at H...
YouR Time...
BAR Time

THE WITCH SHOW
1 Intro Song - Ella Fitzgerald
2 D.T.
3 ALASKA- witch Mix
4 D.T.
5 AMY- Whitney
6 D.T.
7 CHERRI- Bad Karma
8 D.T.
9 VERUCA- Rabbit Heart
10 D.T.
11 SHARON
12 Hocus Pocus (2 Tracks)
13 D.T.
14 ALASKA- Monster Mash
15 D.T.
16 AMY VODKA- Lucia
17 D.T.
18 SHARON- Gladys
19 CHERRI-
20 VERUCA- Haunted Craft
21 SHARON- Metallica
22 ALASKA's ALL- Dreams

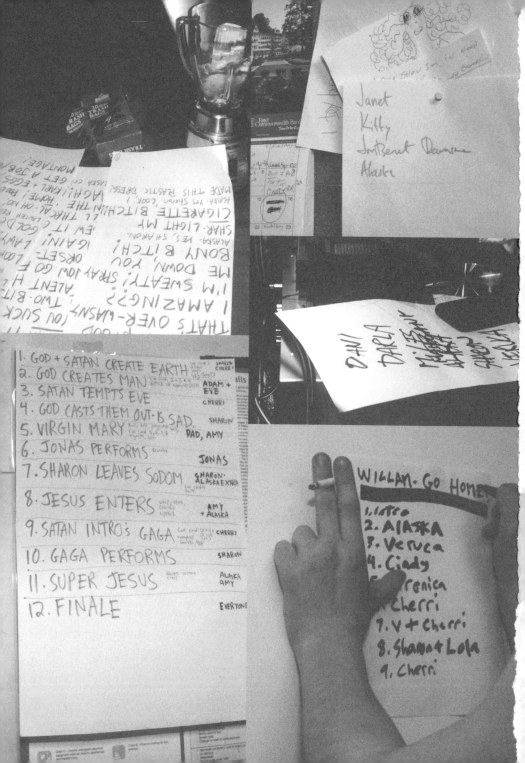

MY NAME'S YOURS, WHAT'S ALASKA?

MY NAME'S YOURS, WHAT'S ALASKA?

A MEMOIR

By ALASKA THUNDERFUCK 5000

with THOMAS FLANNERY

FOREWORD *by* JACKIE BEAT

CHRONICLE BOOKS

SAN FRANCISCO

Names and identifying details of some of the people, events, and places portrayed in this book have
been changed.

Library of Congress Cataloging-in-Publication
Data available.

ISBN 978-1-7972-0322-5
Manufactured in India

Cover photo by Magnus Hastings.
Design by Michael Morris.

Chronicle Books LLC
680 Second Street
San Francisco, CA 94107
www.chroniclebooks.com

10 9 8 7 6 5 4 3 2 1

To my mom, and Lady Gaga, and the Lord almighty. In that order.

I COULD NOT WAIT TO READ THIS BOOK!

And I'm actually friends with Alaska, so that's saying *a lot*. Do I want to read about Lady Bunny? Hell, no! Unless of course, it's her obituary.

All joking aside, I just adore Alaska! She has that very special "can't take your eyes off her" thing that so few stars today seem to possess. Sure, they may have the catch phrase, the signature style, the killer publicist, but how many of them really have "It"? Alaska is probably reading this and thinking, *I don't want Jackie to put other queens down to express her appreciation for me. That's not only harsh, but downright lazy!* Bitch, are you new? Harsh and lazy are the only two special skills listed on my acting resume. They are also what I named my eyebrows, but I'm saving that for *my* book.

Listen, I'm not putting anyone down. I'm just saying that while there are many iconic, popular, and talented Drag artists to come out of *RuPaul's Drag Race*, Alaska is a rare motherfucking magical unicorn, so please, for the love of Ru, shut the fuck up and let me do this.

The moment I first saw Alaska on television I thought, *I like that person!* She just *oozed* something that I was immediately attracted to. And if you're waiting for a cheap, crude bodily fluid joke, I hate to disappoint you. What Alaska so effortlessly and generously *oozed* was, in fact, *Star Power*. Now I'm not sure if *Star Power* is one word, two words, or hyphenated. All I know is that Alaska has it in spades! But the TV camera can be deceiving. For instance, they say it adds ten pounds, so just imagine how truly, annoyingly thin Alaska is in real life. But I'm not here to body-shame one of my best friends. I'm here to say that when I finally met her in real life, she was just as luminous and adorable and naturally entertaining and hilarious as she was on TV. And skinny. Did I mention she's real skinny?

Yes, from the moment we met, it was on. I was thrilled to discover that Alaska had that perfect balance of cattiness and kindness, wickedness and warmth. She was stunningly sexy but also fiercely funny. Honestly, it was like looking in a mirror. Okay, a fun house mirror after dropping acid. But seriously, I felt an instant connection. It probably didn't hurt that she was a huge fan of me and my work. I'm not kidding when I say she knows my material better than I do. But as flattering as that was, it can't sustain a real friendship.

So let me share some of that real friendship with you. Let me give you something you didn't see on *Drag Race*, or hear on *Race Chaser*, or witness at one of her shows. Let me give you a glimpse of the person beneath the ratted wigs, black contacts, and gravity-defying hip pads; the sweet person who is sometimes my daughter, sometimes my sister, and always my friend.

As you no doubt already know, Alaska is a huge *Golden Girls* fan. I am also unnaturally obsessed with the 1980s sitcom about four older women living together in Miami, but Alaska's knowledge of the show puts me to shame. If I attempt to quote an iconic line, I quickly learn that I have merely paraphrased it when Alaska corrects me by properly reciting the line, complete with a dead-on impersonation of the character who orig-inally uttered it. The only time I ever saw her get genuinely pissed off at me was the time my incorrect answer made us lose a *Golden Girls* trivia contest at a Drag-themed hamburger restaurant in West Hollywood—by one point! She will deny it, but she was furious. Remember that less-than-charming person who briefly reared her ugly head during *All Stars*? Well, I met her that night and gurl, it was not cute.

Although we have traveled all over the world together, my favorite, most-treasured memories of spending quality time with Alaska are simple things, like shopping at L.A.'s famed Santee Alley ("Jackie, you *cannot* wear that . . . It's cultural appropriation!") or lunching at our favorite diner in Silver Lake where Alaska always orders at least three beverages. "I'll have a cup of Earl Grey tea, a glass of champagne, and some water, please." I think it's to quench the thirst of her three *Golden Girls*—adjacent personalities: hot tea for her inner Dorothy; sparkling champagne for her inner Blanche; and a simple glass of tap water for her inner Rose. Where's her inner Sophia, you ask? That vindictive, bitter old Sicilian comes out only when Alaska fucks up a challenge or I get a trivia question wrong.

Despite all my snarky shade, I really do love Alaska. When we get together, we talk and laugh and give each other advice, and she often gives me ideas for song parodies. The one thing we don't do is gossip or talk shit about other queens. Oh, trust me, I have tried. But Alaska simply isn't into it. She just listens to me say something bitchy about someone and either ignores it, refusing to take the bait, or, more often than not, chimes in with something positive about the person I'm attempting to read. And that, my friends, is Alaska in a nutshell. I'm not saying she's a total pushover or doesn't have an edge, but she always seems to make a conscious choice to focus on the positive and find the best in a person or situation and celebrate that.

I honestly don't know how she manages to do it . . . because there are some really stupid cunts out there.

Enjoy the book!

JACKIE BEAT

ONE

Don't Play Like a Girl

My sister Brooke used to have a life-size Raggedy Ann doll, hand-made by my grandmother. It was a horrendous thing with big, bottomless black eyes and farmhouse-red yarn hair. The earliest human memory I possess—I must have been three or four—is going into Brooke's room, taking the doll's pinafore dress off her cotton cloth body, and draping it on myself.

Mom remembers this moment, too. She says she was sitting in the kitchen with her best friend, Kim, when I came prancing in, showing off my clever new costume. They both burst into laughter, which is the part of this story I remember most.

"Do you think Justin's gay?" Kim asked my mother.

"I don't know," Mom said.

"He sure does like girls' clothes," Kim said.

Mom tells me she didn't really think much about it. This was the 1980s, and the sexuality of your offspring had yet to become a hot topic of discussion. Such things just didn't occur to most people. As I sashayed out of the kitchen and into the living room, Mom got the mop and placed it on my head. My very first wig.

I grew up in Erie, Pennsylvania, a small town that thinks itself much bigger than it is, due to our coveted peninsula and close proximity to Canada. On 9/11, many citizens of Erie were convinced we were the next logical target for a terrorist attack. Luckily, they were wrong.

Nine months out of the year, Erie is covered in a blanket of snow. The other three months are sweltering and unbearably muggy. The people of Erie will gladly complain to you about these unfavorable conditions. Yet, generation after generation, they refuse to leave. Some say complaining is draining. But as a proud Erie-ite, I say complaining is part of my heritage.

My mother grew up in Erie. Her name is Pamela. She has had three husbands, making her Erie's Elizabeth Taylor. My birth father was husband number one, but husband number two raised me as his own. My two dads both worked in machine shops.

While growing up, Mom's brothers teased her mercilessly because of her height, but as she grew into her stems she became a stunning glamazonian beauty. She's six feet and one inch tall, just like me. I wish I inherited her nose, too, goddammit.

From a very early age I wore glasses. The frames were ever changing because I could never find a pair that looked right on me, or more specifically, on my nose. Maybe it was my whole face that was problematic. Or maybe it was the abysmal selection LensCrafters had to offer in the early 1990s.

It seemed I was always searching for the right look. Especially when it came to my hair. Its natural wave and curl led me to try every hairstyle imaginable: side part, center part, high and tight, buzz cuts. No matter what I did with it, I never felt that my hair looked quite right. Our coexistence has been a lifelong struggle.

My mom's hairdresser worked at a salon inside JCPenney at the Millcreek Mall, and we'd go there regularly together. Tanica was her name.

And no—that is not a fictitious name fabricated to protect her identity. Her name was actually Tanica. Tanica was beautiful, with long, gorgeous blonde hair. She was also—shocker—very tan. I remember sitting in her salon chair one day and sighing deeply. "I wish I could have hair like yours," I said. I saw Tanica shoot my mom a concerned look. Mom just shrugged. I didn't know what the look meant, but I knew I had said something wrong.

Erie has a small amusement park, called Waldameer. One summer night, I won a Mighty Mouse stuffed toy at a ring toss game. When we got home, I decided to give him a makeover. I gave him bright blush on both cheeks with a red crayon.

I showed my mother. "Look! He's pretty!" I said.

My mother screamed, "You ruined him!"

I didn't understand. I thought it was an improvement.

Mom tried to curtail my habits, gently replacing Barbies with trucks and assorted building blocks. Once, at my neighbor's house, I managed to make my way into a play session with some of the girls and got my hands on a Barbie. I slipped her into a 1980s-style mini dress with a sparkly gray chiffon ruffle at the top.

"Boys don't play with Barbies," said one of the girls, as she took the newly accessorized doll out of my hands. Even a child—a particularly bitchy child, but still a child—knew better than to allow one of her curvaceous pieces of plastic to fall into the hands of someone designated a boy. I realized then that I was the one with the problem; everyone else seemed to know their role already.

As I got older, my love for Barbie only grew, though she was out of the question for me. The dolls that belonged to my sister collected dust in a box in her closet, untouched and unused after she outgrew them. Meanwhile I was expected to play with the drab and dismal G.I. Joe. He didn't even have more than one outfit. I could have given Barbie fashion! I could have given her haircuts! I could have given her *life*!

Drawing ended up becoming a constructive outlet for me. Not anything fancy; I didn't have art store supplies, just Bic pens and school pencils. I'd draw my own comic books, with sweeping soap opera narratives set in fantasy universes. Most of the characters were women; I loved drawing the clothes, the hair, the beauty. Through my drawings, these precious feminine things could be mine.

I was always fascinated by women. And spectacle! A defining moment in my young understanding and adoration of "camp" was when Mom took my brother, sister, and me to see Tim Burton's *Batman Returns*. Michelle Pfeiffer's portrayal of Catwoman sent me into a deep adolescent obsession.

Oh dear Goddess . . . Catwoman. I was in love! Her origin story was replete with themes and imagery that would one day feed my own alter ego. Catwoman was once a meek, bespectacled secretary named Selina Kyle. Then her lecherous boss pushed her out of a skyscraper. Little did he know, a herd of stray cats licked Selina's wounds, magically bringing her back to life. She made her way home, pulled a vinyl raincoat from the back of her closet, and haphazardly stitched together a sickening skintight catsuit. Liberated from the cowering, introverted life she left behind, Selina Kyle now took to the streets of Gotham City, exacting murderous revenge on all the men who had wronged her. Catwoman was born!

I can see now why I identified with her so fiercely. Society told her to be quiet and do as she was told. But Selina fought against convention, repurposed uncommon materials into stunning fashions, threw occasional tantrums, and embraced the power that lay dormant inside her.

I was a total Catwoman fangirl. When I'd play outside with my brother, we'd pretend to be superheroes. He would be Batman, and I was always Catwoman. Most of my character play was spent trying to turn trash bags into a catsuit. It's harder than it looks. I'd prance around on my toes and crack my pretend whip. My younger brother, Cory, would torment me, I think because he wanted me to act the way he thought a big brother should. He'd try to get me to throw a ball back and forth with him, but that was just not happening. I only wanted to be Catwoman.

One day, Mom called me into the bathroom. She was doing her hair, which was quite an undertaking. The waft of hair spray was painful to my eyes yet soothing to my senses. Mom sat me on the side of the tub and put down her hair curler.

"Justin, you're a boy, so you have to act like a boy. Don't play like a girl."

Every time I smell Aqua Net I flash back to that moment. I didn't know what it meant to play like a girl, or a boy. I was just playing however came naturally. To have the main caretaker of my life tell me that my way of being was incorrect was a revelation. I knew it was a big deal, that I was finally being let in on some big secret that I had somehow never been told before. That's when it truly dawned on me that my natural instincts were considered wrong.

As hard as it was for my younger self to hear, I now understand that talk Mom had with me. A man wearing a dress was then—and still very much remains—a highly politicized and polarizing action. Mom could see trouble brewing (everyone could see it), and it scared her. She didn't want to see me get hurt. Playing like a girl would bring taunting, alienation, or worse. My mom is emotional, and she's honest, and I fucking love her so much.

Queer kids have to learn quickly that it can be dangerous to act outside the norm. But "nature finds a way," and I found some clever loopholes. When playing superheroes with my brother and his friends, I made up my own hero to play: Cat Man. He was pretty much Catwoman but with different pronouns and a machine gun instead of a whip.

As much as I tried to fit in and hide my girly side, my inner femininity refused to be suppressed. When the huge JCPenney catalog would come in the mail, I would look through the girls' section and plan all the clothes I would wear when I grew up. I'd scan through the models and think, *I'm going to look like her.* This wasn't a wish; there was no yearning. It was just an inevitability. I was going to grow up and be a girl. A woman.

Does that mean I am trans? I don't think so. I don't consider myself to be fully a man or a woman. Maybe I'm a little bit of both. I didn't have the terminology at the time, but *gender nonconforming* was (and remains) the term that best suits me. "Gender floral," as my best friend, Jeremy, says.

As much as I always internally understood that I didn't identify with being a man or a woman, I also understood I needed to hide that. The only place I always felt safe to play freely was Grandma Pierette's house. She was French Canadian, with a glorious accent and a mouth like a sailor. Her expletives were always in French, and we could never get her to admit what they meant. I asked my mom what *putain* meant once, and she laughed and said, "Nothing you need to worry about."

Whenever we went to Grandma Pierette's, my sister and I had free rein to play in her clothes. She had exquisite clothes and things! There were tennis dresses, real fur coats with matching hats, lipsticks in every color, and clip-on earrings, and I can still smell her perfumes: deep, dark bottles of French perfumes with old-fashioned squeeze bulbs.

My sister and I would innocently adorn ourselves in her various pieces and parade around the living room. "Merde!" Grandma Pierette would yell, laughing.

During one of these shows, my father playfully suggested for me the name *Justina*.

My sister teased and laughed at me. "Justina! Justin's a girl!" she said. I felt ashamed and didn't know why. Dad didn't mean it to be mean; he was laughing with me, not at me. Actually it's not a terribly unsuitable Drag name. It's a very one-name diva, like Cher, or Heklina.

The other great thing about Grandma Pierette's? She loved *The Golden Girls*. We'd watch it together every week. I was too young to understand any of it, but the comedic pacing was so tight I knew when to laugh anyway. My favorite episodes were when they'd dress in costumes: Dorothy and Sophia as Sonny and Cher; or when the girls dressed up as chickens for a children's production of *Henny Penny*. Or the one where Dorothy and Blanche sang at the Rusty Anchor. Or the time they went to the gym and a fast-talking aerobics instructor named Yvonne talked them into spending all their money on ridiculous workout clothes. Ah . . . classic.

I'm not sure what would possess a young child to love a show about four older, single women in Miami. But *The Golden Girls* was a comfort to me then, and it still is now. Dorothy was my favorite. She may not have been the most beautiful, but she could slay you with a single punch line, or even just a look. The other girls in the house may have had more dates, but Dorothy always had the last laugh.

TWO

King of Queens

Sophomore year of high school I decided it would be a really great idea to bleach my hair.

It wasn't a decision I came to by myself. My friend Alaina had a penchant for all things cosmetological, and she'd never bleached anyone's hair before. I was her willing, gullible guinea pig.

Alaina came over with a box of drugstore hair dye and a VHS tape of *The Rocky Horror Picture Show*. I had no idea what it was, but from the moment those blood-red lips appeared, I was enthralled. All Alaina told me was that it was a musical. But in this musical, I witnessed a man in heels and makeup openly ogling a muscular blond stud in a gold Speedo.

I was instantly intrigued. The in-your-face sexuality of *Rocky Horror* created a true bond between Alaina and me. We saw ourselves in its cast of freaks: She was Magenta; I was Frank-N-Furter. Just like those lonely creatures from a far-away planet, we were social outcasts, cautiously figuring out how to push back against the mainstream.

As for my hair, things didn't go as well as planned. It wasn't blond exactly; it was more yellow. Egg-yolk yellow. My great-grandmother Nannie came over the next day, and when she saw what we had done to my hair, she took a deep puff on her cigarette, pointed at my head, and hissed out one word: "Ugly."

Nannie wasn't wrong, I'll give her that. But I still liked it, and we had so much fun doing it. Alaina pretty much became my first Drag mother that night. She taught me a lot about hair and makeup, how to use bobby pins, and how to put on lashes. I started reading magazines that Alaina and my mom were reading, like *Cosmopolitan* and *Teen*, always searching for beauty tips. My eyebrows became a particular focus. I started plucking them into an ideal shape, though eventually I plucked them until they were gone. I whitened my teeth and started tanning, dyeing my hair, and wearing homemade colored contact lenses, tinted with food coloring. Anything I could do to alter my appearance.

Alaina also became a convenient alibi when I'd hang out with my first boyfriend: Phillip. At the dawn of the age of the internet, we met in an AOL chat room. He was as tall as me, he had a really high voice, and he had a car.

I introduced my mom to Phillip and told her he was my new friend.

"How did you meet?" Mom asked. It was a valid question; he didn't go to my school. And he was obviously gay, as was I. Something was clearly being left unsaid.

"At the mall," I said, and changed the subject. I thought I was slick. I didn't think anyone else could tell.

The next day Mom brought it up again, but this time she was blunt. "Justin . . . are you a homosexual?" she said.

And I said, "Yes."

Mom told me she loved me and supported me. We cried and we hugged. "As long as you're happy, I'm happy," she said. It was really sweet. Most gay kids can't ask for a much better response. Later she told me a counselor had given her tips on how best to handle the situation, and I guess they gave her good advice because it all worked out. We've always been able to be open and candid with each other.

My sister and younger brother already knew I was gay. They couldn't believe it took Mom so long to put it together. Now that Mom did know, I wasn't so worried about anyone else finding out. I talked to both my fathers, and both responded compassionately. It was such a relief, and I felt like I was finally free of a heavy burden.

Now that I was officially "out," I started to come into myself more. No more oversized bland-colored shirts to hide beneath. My clothes got way tighter. Alaina helped me alter vintage clothes we'd find in thrift stores to make them small enough to fit my absurd proportions. She had a great eye for fashion and incredible taste. She taught me how to express myself by turning throwaway rags into something fashionable and punk.

My coming out happened to coincide with the career debut of one Miss Britney Jean Spears from Kentwood, Louisiana. Publicly, Alaina and I were very much of the notion that "Britney Spears sucks." We still liked her music, *loved* her music, could not stop listening to her music, but we pretended to like it only ironically.

"We are only learning the exact choreography to 'I'm a Slave 4 U' because we're making fun of her," we'd say, trying to convince ourselves more than anyone else. Marilyn Manson was more our style, publicly, and while I totally bonded with the Manson freaks, secretly my heart belonged to Britney. She influenced me on a personal level more than she'll ever know. I vividly remember hearing "Oops! . . . I Did It Again" for the first time on the school bus, and it gave me chills. At the end of the song, when the chorus plays along with the counter chorus, and they sort of weave in and out of each other? It's giving me a tingling sensation right now. The production value!

Like many of my peers, I consumed endless hours of television entertainment, which led me to develop a vague but plausible intuitive understanding that I wanted to become famous. All of my insecurities would disappear, all of my problems would be solved, if only I could get the entire world to fall in love with me. But how? There were no famous people who looked like me or acted like me. No one famous ever came from Erie, Pennsylvania.

Fame would come only if I put the work in. This much was clear. So I focused on what I had within reach: I started taking voice lessons and doing school plays. The lead dropped out of a neighboring town's production of *Joseph and the Amazing Technicolor Dreamcoat*. My voice teacher pulled some strings, and I got the part. It was my first time in a face full of makeup on stage. Joseph becomes the pharaoh at the end of the second act, and I did my own makeup effect for this dramatic transformation. I drew Cleopatra lines with eyelash glue on the sides of my eyes, then covered them in gold glitter and outlined it all in black liquid eyeliner. The backstage moms were reticent to turn over such responsibility to a young student, but when I took the stage looking like the love child of Donny Osmond and Elizabeth Taylor, they were flummoxed, flustered, and flabbergasted.

The next year I played the lead in *The Music Man*, and again, I insisted on taking my makeup plot into my own hands: heavy brown eyeliner, honey-colored tan, slicked hair, caked-on blush. I was giving you Harold Hill meets Sally Bowles. My entire family came to see me bring in "76 Trombones," but I was painted for "Maybe This Time." Even Nannie came!

By senior year of high school, I felt like I knew who I was as a person. I knew I didn't care what people thought about me, I knew I liked playing with the meaning of gender, and I knew I wanted to be an actor. Based on these three personality traits, I also knew I needed to get out of suburban life and into a big city. People in Erie were nice enough and I had plenty of girl friends, but everything seemed so small. I knew there was something bigger out there. I wanted more.

My high school announced prom court a few weeks before the year-end dance. Somehow, I ended up in the running for prom king. The way our school chose prom king and queen was different than most: Girls vote for prom king and boys vote for prom queen. And were the girls going to vote for some guy on the football team who's a dick, or for the guy who sits with them when we're skipping gym class together?

The night of the prom was also the night of my first midnight screening of *Rocky Horror Picture Show*. Alaina agreed to be my date to prom, and we planned to attend both prom and the midnight screening in *Rocky Horror* attire.

Mom cried when she found out, but tears would not deter me. She begged and pleaded with me to attend prom in more traditional garb. I humbly acquiesced and rented a tuxedo. We were able to compromise, and I at least got to pick out a ruffly shirt.

Prom was fine. It was corny, but I had seen *Romy and Michele's High School Reunion*, so I knew how important a prom could be. Alaina looked perfect. Her dress was 1950s style, black with white polka dots. Very old Hollywood pinup. We had a good time, even if we were forcing ourselves to do so.

And then I won prom king. I wasn't surprised, and I wasn't really too excited, either. A lot of the girls had told me they were voting for me, and though I know they were trying to be nice, it wasn't the kind of attention

I was looking for. Alaina couldn't stop laughing when they announced my name. "King?" she said. "King of the queens!" Laughing and laughing. The whole thing seemed so silly. It felt like I was supposed to care about all this, but none of it really mattered to me at all. I felt bad. I'm sure these other kids would have loved to be named prom king, and here I was, acting as though it were beneath me. Was I so empty inside? Wasn't this all supposed to mean something?

There were some boos when I received my crown and scepter, but I pretended I didn't hear them. I did my best to act like a king and not act like a girl onstage. Then I went back to find Alaina.

"Let's get out of here," I said.

"Thank God," Alaina said.

I quickly changed into fishnets and a corset, then drove. Alaina changed into her costume on the way. We took turns caking on white makeup all over each other in the theater parking lot. As we walked in, Alaina let me lean on her. It was my first time in heels. I got the hang of it pretty quickly.

We looked good, and the rest of the attendees loved us. I was having a great time, making new friends and dancing the "Time Warp." I felt truly happy, and it was abundantly clear to me then, dressed as Frank-N-Furter, that I was indeed capable of immense joy, doing what I wanted to do, instead of what others expected me to do.

I got home late and Mom was still up. I told her I'd won prom king, and she cried and hugged me. White powdered makeup rubbed off all over her. I promised her I looked normal in the prom photos. She laughed. "I don't think they've had a prom king like you before," she said. "I'm proud of you." I let her have my crown.

That night I had a very vivid dream. I was standing on stage, with no idea what to do. It sort of felt like the prom, but this dream felt urgent,

like something was coming. I woke up anxious and scared, trying to piece together what it could all mean. Then, it came to me: *Gender is a lie.*

Gender was just some made-up, arbitrary notion that some people have to wear a certain kind of clothing and other people have to wear different kinds of clothing. My whole life, I'd been told what it meant to be a boy, and I had placidly played along. But winning prom king, with the virility and level of masculinity that title represents, meant nothing to me.

I sensed that within me was the power to fight back against the gender construct. Clothing had a lot to do with it. Clothing inherently has immense power. It can change the way a person presents themselves to the world just as easily as it can change the way a person feels in the depths of their soul. Clothing can be dangerous; wearing the wrong piece of clothing, at the wrong time, in the wrong place, can get you killed. *Killed.* Over fabric.

I wasn't particularly interested in presenting as a woman in my day-to-day life. When I'd talk about it with Alaina, I'd laugh and say I had to wear boys' clothes because I needed pockets. But there was also the red-veined fear of what it meant to walk down the street as a woman. As a man, I can easily disappear and go about my life. Women have it hard as fuck out there, under men's leering gaze and perpetual harassment.

I would love to live in a *Star Trek* future where people aren't so hung up on whether the baby is going to wear pink or blue. The human experience could be magically liberated if it wasn't boxed in by all this stuff. What if all the babies just wore green? For nature!

THREE

Higher Education

I was a straight-A student all throughout high school, but I wasn't putting that work in because I cared about AP Algebra; I was doing it because a college scholarship was likely the only chance I had of getting to a big city. And so, with the help of Sallie Mae, I accepted an invitation to attend the University of Pittsburgh, about two hours south of Erie. Mom was sad to see me go but happy I didn't end up in New York.

Before I left for school, I planned my new look. First I raided my grandmother's closet and claimed her vintage clothes as my early inheritance, including a big, ugly fur coat. My hair was shaved on the sides, and long and spiky on top—a real chop shop haircut. It was flamboyant and colorful, which attracted some negative attention around Erie. Groups of kids would laugh and scream at me. In Pittsburgh, I knew things would be different.

Pittsburgh has a surprisingly scrappy, working-class artistic vibe. Andy Warhol, the patron saint of pop art, went to Carnegie Mellon, one of several universities located in Pittsburgh.

Surprisingly, Pittsburgh also has a vibrant gay scene. Little gay dive bars pop up all along the Allegheny River. *Queer as Folk,* one of the first gay-themed shows on television, was based in Pittsburgh. Maybe because it's a college town, with a big youth population. Every year brought a huge influx of musical theater and dance students into Pittsburgh, each with a sizable number of queers. U of Pitt had an LGBT alliance on campus, which I happily attended, as it was one of the only ways for those of us under twenty-one to meet each other.

At the time, bars and clubs were some of the only safe spaces for queers to congregate. One of the most popular bars in Pittsburgh was called Pegasus, famous for its eponymous Miss Pegasus pageant. Pegasus also had under-twenty-one nights. I would go there a lot with Jeremy, a friend I made sitting in the front row of Psychology 101. My first real gay friend, Jeremy was half deaf and wore a hearing aid but was a great listener. We went to Pegasus one night, and there was a Drag queen performing. Or rather, she was pretending to sing along to a Madonna song.

"What is this?" I asked Jeremy. "Does she think we don't know she's not really singing?"

"It's called lip-syncing, that's what Drag queens do."

Jeremy was ever so slightly older than me, so he showed me the ropes. He was a real working-class queer, living on student loans and microwave ramen noodles. His family members were mostly coal miners, but Jeremy was a music savant with a hefty scholarship.

We usually wound up at Pegasus. We never missed an under-twenty-one night. Sometimes we'd go to a bar called New York, New York, a dive frequented by older men. They didn't card, and the daddies were more than willing to flirt and buy us drinks. We'd find ways to get drunk. At the end of the night we'd walk home, holding each other up.

Neither Jeremy nor I had existed as gay men without being under the

watchful eyes of our family. Now that we found ourselves away from home, it was great to have a partner in crime, in case things went too far. When we were being well-behaved, Jeremy and I would stop in at the LGBT alliance and play nice. But when we were being bad, we'd get drunk on the cheapest liquor we could find and take a treacherous bus ride downtown to Pegasus or Images or Lucky's (which had strippers).

There's an incredible, deep ravine that separates the University of Pittsburgh from Carnegie Mellon. Right on its precipice once stood Holiday, another of our main watering holes. They had fifty-cent draft beer nights, which always got us wasted, and '80s night, which also got us wasted. One night at Holiday, I started viciously hitting on some guy, who was there with his unamused boyfriend.

I'm not a violent person, but I do have a big mouth. Especially when I'm wasted on fifty-cent draft beer. I was talking shit and making it very clear I was interested in this guy.

"Leave my man alone or I'm going to punch you in the face," the boyfriend said, and he was serious. He pushed me in the chest and I stumbled
backward.

I got so scared, like in the episode of *The Golden Girls* when the girls
find themselves wrongfully imprisoned for prostitution and come face-
to-face with a disgruntled hooker in their jail cell. "Punch? Heavens!" I
clutched my jacket together, dropped a barstool between us, and took off.

Jeremy and I ran out of the bar just in time, stumbling and laughing.
We ended up walking down Forbes Avenue in Oakland, around the university center. There was a 7-Eleven there. In the parking lot, smoking a
cigarette, stood this person you couldn't fucking miss: leopard-print pants
and punked-out, multicolored hair.

"That's Nix N. Kutts," Jeremy said, watching me gawk.

I'd heard of Nix N. Kutts from social media; he was something of a local nightlife celebrity. "Why haven't we seen him around?" I said.

"He's not into gay bars. I think I saw her at Upstage once. She's got another scene. Some weird anarchist commune."

I could get into that, I thought.

I wanted to meet this mysterious creature and find out more, but I didn't dare approach him. I was way too drunk. I remember thinking, *If it is meant to be, I'm sure our paths will cross again.*

Jeremy and I got to my apartment late, around 2 a.m. As I unlocked the door, a car slowly drove by. The passenger window rolled down, and Jeremy and I both peered hard, trying to see who it was.

"Faggots!" A glass bottle smashed at our feet, and the car sped off.

I looked at Jeremy, suddenly feeling sober.

"Should we call the cops?" he asked.

"And tell them what?"

"Whoever that was knows where you live," he said.

What were the cops going to do? I had no idea what to even tell them.

We got inside, locked the door, and turned off the lights. Jeremy set up a sleeping bag on the floor, and we both tried to sleep. I was scared, deeply scared.

"Did I make the wrong choice moving to Pittsburgh? Maybe I should have gone to New York," I said.

"You can't run from hate, you'll find it wherever you go. Hate is part of human nature."

"Human male nature," I said.

"Fuck 'em all," we said in unison. As the sun came up, I fell asleep.

FOUR

Shakespearean Drag

My major in college was theater arts. I couldn't get into any of the schools that had dedicated programs for acting, but it was a blessing in disguise. At Pitt, I learned how to hang lights, use a power drill, design costumes—and I took acting classes, too. We had a "director exchange" program, and a Russian director came in to put on a production of Shakespeare's *Pericles*. It's not a play that's done often; it's a long, meandering story that just goes on and on. Not to offend Shakespeare, but *Pericles* is kind of boring. Not a very good show. Plus it's massive in scale; there's a pirate ship at sea and giant castles in various far-flung locales to create. Only someone with a massive, unchecked ego would dare to helm such a production. What college program wants to go through all that trouble?

But this Russian director, who barely spoke any English, insisted on doing *Pericles*. He was at least eighty years old and terrifyingly strict. He held a group audition, and I tried out for a small role: Pirate Number Three. I read a couple of lines and he stopped me.

"No, you, this," he said. He picked up a script and scribbled down my role: Bawd, the whorehouse madam.

I started to recite the lines.

"Higher voice! Like woman!" the director screamed.

I went higher.

"Higher! Higher!"

He was such an imposing force of a man, I didn't dare say no. I screeched out my lines as loudly as my falsetto allowed, and he was finally satisfied. The role of Bawd was mine.

When Shakespeare was alive, all the female roles would have been played by a man in Drag. And it wasn't because Drag was fierce and fun; it was the law. Theater people were considered to be sexually promiscuous, on par with whores and circus folk. Women weren't allowed to be part of that world; it was much too uncouth. Though such laws were inherently misguided, they unknowingly shaped the historical tradition of female impersonation. Imagine the original premiere of *Romeo and Juliet*, some four hundred years ago, with those "star-crossed lovers" both played by men. And *everyone* went to see these romance dramas. It definitely puts some perspective on classic plays by Shakespeare and his contemporaries.

The Bawd was a really rotten character, and my costume was a scary-ass Drag version of a medieval wench: full-body padding, with huge boobs. The biologically born females in our theater department were not thrilled with my casting, since the ratio of male to female theater majors versus male to female characters in plays was wildly askew. But our tyrannical Russian director was not much for group decision-making. I was the whorehouse madam, and that was final. I had so much fun with it, and it was technically the first time I performed in Drag on a stage.

The show wasn't very well received. The school paper's review said it was an overblown waste of money. But the review *did* say that I was "physically articulate," which sounded like a compliment. They also said they couldn't understand anything I was *saying* because I was "shrieking" in such a high falsetto.

After *Pericles* ended, I was aching to have a real Drag experience, which meant going out to a bar in Drag. Alaina was coming down to visit me for a couple of days, and I asked her if she could make me pretty.

"This I promise you," she said.

Alaina brought me a basic blonde wig with bangs. "It looks deflated," I said. "I want it to be bigger!"

"Of course we're going to make it bigger, but there's a process."

We teased up the wig to make it as big as we could. I didn't have any clothes to wear, and we had no money to buy anything, so we decided to make a dress out of whatever we had on hand. After assessing our possibilities, I took three black trash bags, cut the bottoms out of each of them, and attached them to each other with duct tape to form one giant trash bag tube. Then I stepped into the tube dress and taped it to my body, paying special attention to the waist, which Alaina helped me cinch in. Then I put a slit up the leg, which I reinforced with duct tape to keep it from ripping all the way up. And finally, I created straps out of duct tape. That was it! I'd made my first trash bag dress, and I've basically been wearing the same outfit ever since! (Note: I've since learned the hard way that whatever color you choose, make sure the trash bags are unscented. The scent may be pleasing in a trash can, but it will most definitely make you vomit if it's all over your body.)

With Alaina's help, my trash bag dress looked like a million bucks. We finished my look with a dark, smoky eye, and then we bobby-pinned my now extra-large blonde wig onto my head.

It was a Tuesday night, not even a weekend or anything. But I looked great. This was my moment. "The beginning of the rest of your life," as RuPaul says. It was going to be my grand entrance into the world of Drag, with a capital *D*. We got to the bar, ran inside (literally, I was basically naked and it was cold out), and waited for gagged gays to drop to the floor in real, actual death drops.

Well, the death drops never came. The bar itself was dead. There were maybe five people in attendance. None of them even looked up.

Alaina and I didn't care. I wasn't really doing Drag for anyone else; I was doing it for myself. This was meant to be a trial run for being in Drag in a public setting. We got drunk and made friends with the bartender, so in my mind it was a success. My trash dress held together the whole night, and I considered that a massive victory in itself.

I felt like I'd experienced . . . something. I wasn't sure what. Getting ready with Alaina was the best part of the night. It felt like sisterhood. Like some sacred ritual of beauty.

I didn't need money to do Drag, and I didn't need to be especially talented. It was a medium that allowed me to express myself using whatever I had on hand. Drag was calling to me, as if I were a moth, slowly floating up to a shiny spinning disco ball.

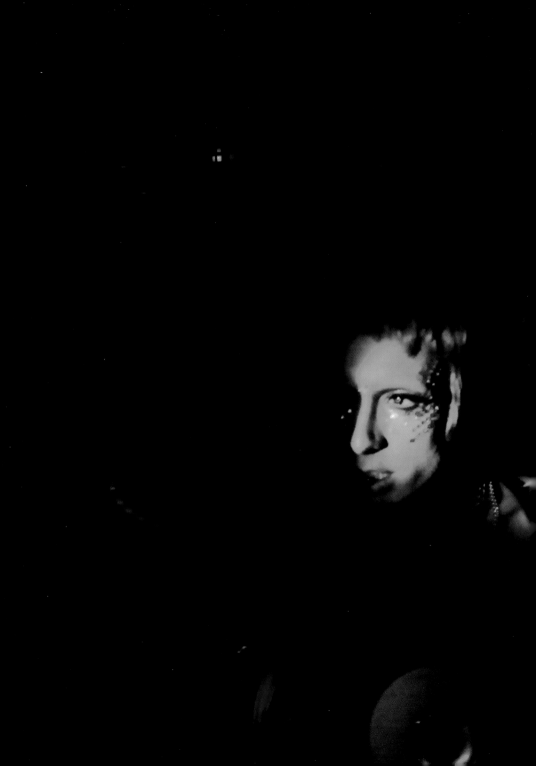

FIVE

Tr*nnyshack

My senior year, Jeremy moved to Los Angeles for grad school at UCLA.

During my last spring break, I spent a week sleeping on Jeremy's couch in Hollywood, to see what L.A. was like. I was pondering whether or not to move out there when I graduated, to try my luck at being a real actor.

L.A. was all right. Sort of like New Jersey, but with palm trees. Lots of malls. We went to Santa Monica Boulevard in West Hollywood and did our own bar crawl down the strip of gay bars.

By the end of the night, I felt unimpressed. I was expecting so much more, and while surely the quantity of gay life was elevated, the quality was not much different than I'd seen in Shadyside, the respectable boutique gay neighborhood in Pittsburgh.

"Let's go to San Francisco for the weekend. We're already in California and I bet they have better bars there," I said.

"That's like an eight-hour car ride," Jeremy said.

"Perfect, I'll bring my Britney CDs."

It was a lovely drive up the coast. We found an inordinately cheap hostel and made our way to Golden Gate Park. Jeremy was able to find pot easily, and we just sat in the park and smoked a joint. I remember feeling like I could really relax there. A vibe of abiding peace.

We started talking to a local leather daddy, who told us if we were really in town to see San Fran's best bar scene, we should stay in town a couple of days longer so we could check out the hot Tuesday night party, Tr*nnyshack. It was at a bar called the Stud, which was a leather bar every other night of the week, but on Tuesdays it was "for young queerdos like you," he said.

That sounded good enough for me. Our trip was extended.

Tuesday night we showed up early and thank God because the place was packed. I was in tight jeans and the tightest shirt I could possibly fit on my body. Converse All Stars. And my hair was in a side swoop in the front, kind of like Justin Bieber. In the back was a mullet.

A little after midnight the show started. The show's host, Heklina, came out and informed us that every week Tr*nnyshack had a different theme, and the theme of the evening was Duran Duran! Each performer would be doing a lip-sync number by the quintessential '80s heartthrobs.

Heklina's hair was larger than any queen I'd seen before, her makeup gaudier and more over the top than I ever thought possible. I was enthralled. She was wearing what looked like a chauffeur's uniform, but it was made of pleather, complete with a pleather bell cap. After her opening remarks, she went right into a lip-sync performance of Duran Duran's "The Chauffeur." I couldn't believe a Drag queen was going to lip-sync to a male vocal. Wasn't that against the rules?

As the backing track for her song began, Heklina pulled out a cardboard cutout of a convertible and pretended to drive around the stage. It was simple, but effective, and cheap! And the audience ate it up! I ate it up! This kind of Drag looked accessible, like anyone could do it. And more importantly, it looked fun.

Something cracked open inside me at Tr*nnyshack that night. I thought I knew what Drag was, but this was something completely different.

Twelve different Drag queens each performed Duran Duran lip-syncs, and just like Heklina, each one of them had a fully realized narrative that went along with the song. None of them were concerned with glamour or polish. They were in your face, visceral, and shocking. They were paying homage to Duran Duran, but really they were mocking the absurdity of '80s glamour at the same time. Each girl had bigger tits, higher hair, and more makeup than the queen who came before. I mean huge, water balloon tits, oversized paint, and piles, piles of hair, made up of several wigs tied together to form these heinously large monstrosities.

Tr*nnyshack was a pivotal moment in my life because it was the first time I saw a future for myself in Drag. Drag was subversive, a genderfuck form of artistic expression. They weren't trying to look like women. They were trying to fuck with gender and the concept of beauty. It didn't matter if you were really good at makeup or if you were a giant hairy dude; you could make magic happen with Drag. It was like they were taking pop culture, flipping and inverting it, chewing it up, turning it queer, and spitting it back out again. It wasn't lofty or unattainable; it was for everyone. It didn't matter if you had money or an education.

After the show, I told Jeremy: "I'm going back to Pittsburgh, and I'm bringing this whole vibe with me." And that's exactly what I did.

SIX

The Fish Bowl

Chi Chi LaRue, the legendary Drag queen and porn director, was coming to Pittsburgh. I saw the flyer for her show: *The Fish Bowl Contest, $250 prize.* Contestants had to perform a lip-sync to whatever random song they picked out of a fish bowl on stage. It was a real gamble; you could end up with a song you knew well, or one you didn't know at all.

I knew a lot of songs. And for someone literally counting pennies, $250 was an unheard-of amount of money. I picked up the flyer and called Alaina. Into my oversized Nokia cell phone I said, "I'm going to do this contest and I'm going to win." I'd really done Drag only the one time, but after seeing Tr*nny-shack I was *motivated*. I already had a Drag name picked out: Alaska Thunderfuck. It was a potent strain of weed that I knew was meant to be my Drag name the first time I heard it.

Around this time, I had just started dating this older guy named Travis. Barely dating, we'd slept together two times, and all I knew about him was that his job involved furniture. But I liked him. I told him about the contest, and he was adamantly against it.

"If I see you in Drag, I won't be physically attracted to you anymore," he whined, drawing a glitter line in the sand.

This was pretty much what I expected being a Drag queen would be like, so I wasn't totally surprised. Even after all the breakthroughs I'd felt I'd gone through in terms of being comfortable with myself, I still had a deep-seated fear of being perceived as feminine or flamboyant. Of being gay. No matter how hard I tried to convince myself otherwise, part of me simply cared too much about what other people thought of me. And though I don't think I was doing it consciously, I was self-suppressing my personality in order to maintain even the slightest aura of masculinity. Deep down, there was a truer, even gayer me, who remained hidden.

I told Travis I'd think about what he'd said, but later that night I got drunk and called him up: "Fuck you, I'm doing the Fish Bowl Contest. If you don't want to see me in Drag, then you better not show up."

Travis didn't get a chance to respond before I hung up. I felt like Whitney Houston, with every woman all in me. Was I really going to suppress myself for the gratification of someone else? And if being myself meant being absurd and weird and outrageously gay, I might as well just lean into that. Be extra gay, and right up in your face about it.

I was living with roommates in a slum of an apartment. Rent was dirt cheap, which was great, but we had rats and bugs and black mold, which was not so great. Despite all, I was happy, and now I had a mission: to be named the next Miss Fish Bowl. First, I needed a workspace. I found a giant door in a trash pile outside and put it on top of a couple of old filing cabinets from Goodwill. It was my first real desk, from which I could put together my look for the contest. I bought whatever cheap wigs I could find from thrift shops and Halloween stores, and started playing with how

to style them. There would be spraying, there would be teasing, but mostly there was safety-pinning. If a wig wasn't big enough, I'd just add another wig to it. It didn't matter if they matched or not, I just needed bigger hair. I even stuffed them with plastic bags to give the wigs the bloated, busting-at-the-seams look I wanted.

For the performance, I thought about what I'd learned at Tr*nny-shack and came up with a provocative yet simple act I could do, no matter what the song was. This was a Chi Chi LaRue contest; if any Drag queen could appreciate the importance of shock value in a performance, it would be the literal queen of porn.

All the best Drag queens in Pittsburgh showed up for the Fish Bowl, hungry for that cash prize. No one made that kind of money on a normal night of Drag.

As soon as I walked in, I saw Travis and his mortified face, which made me laugh. "Hi, what are you doing here?" I said to him.

"I didn't think you'd really do it," he said.

I thought I'd feel some sort of shame when I saw him, but I didn't. His reaction was oddly gratifying. I shrugged and kept it moving. I didn't want to date some insecure asshole who was scared of a man in a dress. We never spoke again.

When it was my turn on stage, I demurely bowed to Chi Chi and picked my song out of the fish bowl: "How Many Licks?" by Lil' Kim.

"Is it a song you know?" Chi Chi said.

I grabbed the microphone. "Every single word," I said. I lived for Lil' Kim. This had to be a good sign.

For my costume, I had bought a one-dollar black plastic tablecloth and made it into a long dress. As the intro to "How Many Licks?" began, I reached up the dress and pulled out a giant can of beer I'd taped inside. I cracked it open and toasted the crowd, all while lip-syncing flawlessly.

When the second verse started, I dropped the can, reached up my dress again, pulled out a massive double-sided dildo, and twirled it around, like a floppy light saber.

The next verse: I squatted down and birthed a plastic baby.

It was going well; the crowd was on my side and Chi Chi was gagging. As the chorus played out and my performance was coming to an end, I ripped open my skirt to reveal neon painted letters that read: I HEART CHI CHI. I bowed and left the stage, feeling like a winner.

After all the queens performed, Chi Chi brought us all back on stage and judged us based on audience reactions and applause. The crowd screamed out for me, and Chi Chi declared me the official "Miss Fish Bowl." The title was mine, the crown was mine, the $250 was mine, and I even got a little beta fish in a round fish bowl as a bonus prize. My Drag career had started as a massive success.

Winning that contest made me feel like I was hot shit. It was the inciting incident that crystalized in my mind that I could actually be a successful Drag queen. Sometimes I wonder, if I hadn't won, would I have felt so compelled to pursue a life of Drag? Probably. Alaska was a part of me that had been waiting to come out. But winning the Fish Bowl contest felt like, for the first time in my life, I was in the right place at the right time. That had to mean I was on the right path.

SEVEN

Britney, Bitch

I love Britney Spears.

My mean-girl obsession turned into full-on diva worship by my senior year of college. It wasn't so much her talent or what she had to say that drew me to her; she had this *essence*, a mix of youthful innocence and heightened sexuality. Turns out, this essence wasn't something God-given; Britney was very much a man-made product. It was never actually about Britney as an individual; she was a vessel for marketing primal feminine sexual energy on an international scale.

I've always felt drawn to femininity and feminine sexuality. A lot of people are.

Now out of her early stage, Britney was still residing at the pinnacle of her fame but also starting to go off the rails. The whole Hollywood party-girl thing wasn't exactly the height of glamour, but it was everything I wanted out of life. Britney, Lindsay, and/or Paris could be seen stumbling out of nightclubs, clutching tiny purses and cigarettes, with matted blonde hair and sweaty spray tans. *I wanted to be that girl!* Superficial culture was turning into filth, and I was very much here for it. This was me. This was my style.

I liked being flamboyant and colorful. I was still wearing my grandmother's vintage clothes tailored to be skintight on my body, with my big white fur coat on top. My hair was a sort of fauxhawk, shaved on the sides and long and spiky on top. My style may have been on trend in Los Angeles, but in Pittsburgh I was not exactly appreciated as a fashionista. I was starting to get tired of being called a faggot while walking down the street.

I always knew I wanted to be in a big city, and it was clear Pittsburgh wasn't big enough. Graduation was coming up, and I had to decide what to do with myself. All things considered, Los Angeles, the land of sunshine and broken dreams, was starting to sound nice.

Even though I'd now officially done Drag only once, I was pretty sure I was the best Drag performer in all of Pittsburgh. Pegasus was holding their annual Miss Pegasus Pageant, and I signed myself up. I had no idea what a pageant was when I entered, but I was sure it would come naturally to me.

The night of Miss Pegasus, the first thing I noticed was that I was underdressed. All the other contestants were wearing ball gowns; I was dressed as a circus freak, wearing a leopard-skin bra and barely there loincloth, with big black hair and strappy shoes that were two sizes too small.

Pageant queens, I quickly found out, are a very put-together bunch. Pretty much the opposite of Alaska Thunderfuck in every possible way. I'd seen them at Pegasus; I just didn't know the terminology. To a pageant queen, Drag was a career pursuit. These girls were provided with opportunities to travel, get their name known, and make a living. It was consistent work, which I didn't even know was an option. Pageant queens have a high level of reverence for Drag and unmatched respect for its traditions.

There are a lot of rules and regulations, most of it stuff you could learn only through working in the community.

Despite my clear misunderstanding of the assignment, the other competitors were nice to me, very much in a "bless your heart" kind of way. My look was so unfortunate, and I didn't even have blonde hair. I didn't feel like Alaska without blonde hair. I sat in a corner sulking while the other girls took their turns on stage.

"Are you Alaska Thunderfuck?"

I looked up to see this beautiful queen, her makeup perfect, her evening gown flowing all the way down to the floor. "Do I know you?" I said.

"You won the Chi Chi LaRue contest, didn't you?"

"Yes, I did!"

"Yes, you did. All my friends thought I'd won the contest. People were calling me for a week asking why I'd gone out on stage with such *terrible* eyebrows."

I could sort of see why people confused us. If I didn't have big crazy drawn-on eyebrows, yes, maybe we could be twins, or at the very least sisters. We were both tall, tall and skinny, with similar facial structures and extreme amounts of makeup. And her look was edgier than the other girls. She cleaned up nice, but I could tell she'd been able to put her entire ensemble together on the cheap. And based on her overwhelming attitude, I had a feeling she was a bit of a punk underneath it all.

Our slight confrontation didn't break my focus.

For the talent portion of the pageant, I stuck with my circus theme. My favorite part of the circus is the snacks, so I changed into a cotton candy–inspired dress, with pink tulle and carnival balloons in my bra. This real buff guy I knew volunteered to play my sleazy circus strong man, and he put me on a chain and leash. He peacocked around the stage, pimping me out as my lip-sync music started: "Maneater" by Nelly

Furtado. I thrashed around on my leash until the end of the song, when I finally broke free and retaliated by ripping open this guy's stomach to reveal SpaghettiOs blood and guts.

I thought it was cool, maybe a little messy and under-rehearsed. The crowd wasn't into it. They were mostly confused by this tragic creature making a mess on their stage. I exited stage left to a polite smattering of applause.

My doppelgänger came on next. Veruca la'Piranha was her name, according to the show's host. Now, this bitch Veruca was something else. She was wearing some Oktoberfest schoolgirl ensemble, complete with baying backup dancers dressed as sheep who transformed into "Oops! . . . I Did It Again" schoolgirls. I didn't know much about fashion, but this was a moment. There was yodeling, there were *Sound of Music* singalongs, there was Gwen Stefani's "Wind It Up"— it all worked together, and it was all fantastic. This bitch wasn't just telling a story; she had a whole novel.

Watching Veruca lip-sync, I quickly realized that I was not, in fact, the best Drag queen in Pittsburgh. I wasn't even the most original or clever hometown girl. Far from it. Veruca's performance was *electric*. She performed at maximum power, using every bit of the stage. And though we did look alike in a lot of ways, her makeup, hair, and performance were at a level of polish and precision I had never come close to achieving.

The audience rightfully gave Veruca a standing, thunderous ovation. "Great job," I yelled out to her as she passed me backstage. She smiled and winked.

Veruca took first place by a landslide and was named Miss Pegasus 2007. I came in dead last and, in my mind at least, was named Dumbest Drag Queen in Pittsburgh. I got to speak to Veruca again in the dressing room and asked her if she had any advice for a budding young queen with a dream.

"Girl, you came out for evening gown in ripped fishnets and had party balloons in your bra all night."

"So what? What does that mean?" I said.

"Honestly, I think you should have gotten second place. But you're at the wrong venue. This is pageant."

That made sense, I guess. My lip-sync was killer, but it wasn't glamorous. Veruca didn't have to sacrifice her performance art in order to look beautiful. She told a whole story with just a *look*.

I asked Veruca if I could hold her crown. She politely declined, but we exchanged social media handles and became Myspace pen pals.

Soon after the contest, Britney Spears shaved her head. It was a major event in every circle of the news media. CNN had breaking news headlines. Was Britney having a mental breakdown? Some said her career was over. Some passionately cried out that she should be left alone. To me,

shaving off her beautiful hair was the coolest thing Britney had ever done. She was fearlessly rebelling against a system that wanted to sell her as a sex object until they'd bled her dry. They expected her to be pretty and perfect at all times.

Maybe it wasn't pretty, but I thought Britney looked fucking awesome with a buzz cut. That moment I truly became a lifelong stan.

It was coming up on summertime, which meant it was time to graduate and time for Pride festivities. I finally decided to move to Los Angeles, where it would always be summer. Jeremy offered to let me stay with him.

For what I deemed to be my going-away performance, I got myself a slot performing at Pegasus. Who knew what L.A. would bring? This could be the last time I'd perform in Drag.

I did a lip-sync to Britney's "Do Somethin'," a bonus track from her greatest hits album. It is not one of her more popular songs, but it is an absolutely perfect Drag queen number. Only the real hard-core Britney fans knew what I was doing, but it didn't matter if they knew the song or not. It was just about fun, and I was having fun enough for everyone in the room.

At the end of the song, I picked up a pair of clippers and pretended I was shaving my wig. The audience started laughing and clapping, the image of Britney hitting that car with her umbrella still fresh in their brains. Then, as I clipped away, I turned around and removed my wig, revealing my own actual, freshly shaved head underneath.

The crowd went nuts, jumping up and down, throwing dollar bills in my direction. It felt so good because I was sure I was doing exactly what I was supposed to be doing. Performing Drag the right way was like getting high, and the reaction of the audience was instantly addicting.

I ran into Veruca the next day at a Pride event. She was looking like a fashion magazine spread as usual. I was wearing a basic wig, roller skates, and a children's Batman cape.

"A little birdie told me you just shaved your fucking head," Veruca said.

"Yeah, I did, why?"

Veruca ripped off her wig to reveal that her head was freshly shaved, too. I ripped off my wig as well.

"We really are twins," I told her.

Freshly shaven in solidarity with Britney. The living embodiment of feminine sexual energy, spitting in the face of ingrained, malignant machismo.

That is who I am; I am her. She is me.

EIGHT

At the very last minute, I decided I didn't want to do Drag in L.A. I was already through the security line, and I opened up my bags and took all my wigs out of my luggage. Jeremy picked me up at LAX in a borrowed car, and I let him know.

"Was the plane ride that bad?" he asked.

"This might be my only chance to make it as a legitimate actor, so I have to take my shot."

That's what I'd convinced myself of. I was so hungry to be famous it was making me act a little nutty.

Our apartment was in West Hollywood on Laurel. It was small but rent was cheap, and that's all I cared about. Neither of us had any money. Jeremy's grad school course load was dense, but we had good times together. I got a job at a coffee shop while Jeremy was in school. We'd get home around the same time and stay up late smoking weed, watching YouTube clips of Stevie

Nicks and Fleetwood Mac. We were obsessed. Sometimes Jeremy would plug in his Roland electric piano, and we'd sing our favorite songs together.

One late night, as we worked our way through a boisterous rendition of Dolly Parton's "Jolene," there was a loud bang on our apartment door. It was the LAPD, summoned by a disgruntled neighbor. We promised to keep it down. They promised to come back if we didn't.

After they were gone, I yelled, loud enough for any neighbors to hear, "If you don't like Dolly Parton, why don't you make a request!"

We waited for an answer, but none came. Perhaps they just wanted to hear "The Sound of Silence."

I didn't really know much about being an actor in Hollywood, but I assumed it was a life of living cheap, which I was used to. But acting is about other things, too. For 99 percent of actors, it's about getting head-shots, which is literally just a photo of your head, blown up to 8x10. Actors then send postcards of these headshots—in bulk mailings—to agents and casting associates, all of whom will probably immediately throw them in the garbage.

What a headache. What a hassle! Proper headshots, by the way, cost upwards of five hundred dollars. I literally had about five dollars to my name. Jeremy offered to take pictures of me, so I'd at least have something.

"Should I take my labret piercing out for my head shot?"

Jeremy shrugged.

"Should we wait until my eyebrows grow in?" I asked him.

Jeremy shrugged again. "What kind of look are you going for?" he said.

Taking these headshots suddenly turned into an existential crisis. I thought I looked cool by my own standards, but now I was hyperaware that I was not what Hollywood was looking for. To be an actor, you had to look as standard and conventional as possible. It was up to the director to tell you what to wear and how to cut your hair.

I could feel myself resisting, impulsively. The whole process just repulsed me. If I couldn't even figure out how to take one picture of myself, I was not cut out to be an actor. Oh, at all.

Before I ever went on a single audition, I gave up on my dream of being an actor. But it wasn't disheartening; it was more a revelation. The conventional, predicable Hollywood path was not going to work for me. Acting had been a dream job, but not a realistic one. I didn't have the work ethic, I didn't have the ability to withstand constant rejection, and I definitely didn't have the right haircut.

L.A. was still a great city. It was beautiful and sunny every day, and there was a bus system that actually was usable. Well, better than in Pittsburgh, at least. I decided to stick it out a bit longer and see what I could make of myself.

As I pondered where to exert my future energy, I kept coming back to Drag. Drag was performance, it was political, and it was within reach. Drag had given me a way to rebel against the rules of fashion, good taste, and propriety. And since the standards and practices of Hollywood were so grotesque to me, what better way to utterly reject their demands than Drag?

There was no good reason to do Drag and plenty of reasons not to do it. There was no money in it. There was no real model for success as a Drag queen. There was RuPaul, sure. She was the "Supermodel of the World," but at the time she was far off the radar and no other queen had been able to capture the attention of the nation in the way she had.

If I did Drag, really did Drag, I'd likely never have sex again. No one would want to date me. Drag was messy and weird and alienated you from your friends. Despite all that, I could still feel Drag calling out to me. I had this lofty idea that it could be a vehicle for me to be famous. So often I would think to myself, *If only I could be famous, it would fix everything.*

I'd never have to worry about money again. My mother would never have to worry about anything either.

If I was going to do this, *really* do this Drag thing, I would need to figure some things out. Like, how to turn my crusty busty Drag into something at least a little bit pretty. This was L.A. after all! There was a clear vision in my head of what I wanted my Drag to look like; in fact I had been drawing it since high school. This sexy space warrior character, grungy and dirty yet sickening, in killer stilettos, and basically naked except for skimpy straps and underwear. I would wear things that were too small, underwear and strips of fabric that barely covered anything. The apocalypse is quite warm, and long gone are the outdated notions of modesty and good taste.

I wanted to shock people; I wanted to be jarring and kind of scary. But shock value was not a common trait among the queens I saw in Los Angeles. They were like the pageant queens in Pittsburgh, only they were even fiercer and more polished. They could dance bolder and lip-sync tighter, all while radiating hyperfeminine sexuality. There's never been a shortage of Drag queens in Los Angeles; every year a new crop of young, hungry girls shows up, and they all want to be the fiercest and the best.

That was far, far, *far* from my own coming-to-L.A. story, and a galaxy away from my idea of Drag. But Drag was a craft that needed to be worked at and perfected. If I wanted to be an L.A. queen, I'd at least have to try to improve my basic Drag skills. Like, for example, my makeup. The only makeup training I'd had was from theatrical performances in high school and college. Alaina had done my makeup a couple of times, but she'd never really shown me what to use or how to use it. Every time I'd done Drag so far I'd used makeup by Ben Nye, which was bought at costume shops. I had no idea how real human beings did their makeup, let alone how Drag queens were supposed to do theirs.

I went to the drugstore, and for the first time I bought real, drugstore-brand makeup that any other woman would buy. I remember rummaging through lip glosses and thinking, *Women use lip gloss, and I will, too.* It was something so small, but lip gloss was a revelation for me. Not because the makeup was any good for my Drag (you need high-quality makeup to cover up beard stubble), but because I had decided to finally put some effort into what my Drag aesthetic could be.

I had no interest in doing Drag to try to look like a beautiful woman; my Drag would present a heightened caricature of femininity. I mean literally heightened because I would wear the highest heels I could possibly find. And blonde hair, ratted out on top. And a strong black eyeliner. If I wasn't in a blonde wig with a strong eyeliner, I didn't feel entirely like Alaska, and so now I made a promise to myself to never leave Alaska without her signature style.

Alaska didn't come from the outside in; Alaska is Justin, just in different clothes. What else would she be? It's not like she's some alien taking over my body. Or *is* she . . . ?

NINE

Tr*nnyshack Revisited

The most successful queen in L.A. was Jackie Beat, a.k.a. the Queen of Drag, a.k.a. the Inventor of Everything. Jackie Beat was working constantly, running shows all across the city. Her style was a sickening mixture of beauty and camp: Divine meets West Hollywood. Her talents were plentiful; she was an amazing singer and bitingly hilarious, with a razor-sharp wit. Jackie's particular talent was cleverly changing the lyrics to a popular song to make them about big dicks, necrophilia, or scat play. "Hit Me with Your Best Shot" became "Text Me with a Cock Shot." "Smooth Operator" became "Poo on Me Later." You know, wholesome family stuff. Audiences loved it, and her shows always brought in the biggest crowds.

At Here Lounge in WeHo, I came across a flyer for a Drag contest, judged by Jackie Beat. It was a lip-sync contest, and performers could choose any song they wanted. Easy money, I figured. I could just copy the same winning act I did for Chi Chi LaRue in Pittsburgh. The queens of Los Angeles would never know what hit them!

The night of the contest, I came prepared with a tablecloth dress and a burned CD of "How Many Licks," figuring it was basically my signature song. As my performance started and Lil' Kim's iconic rap verses spewed forth, I went through all the same motions I did last time: I pulled out the beer, then the double-sided dildo, and then my plastic baby popped out of my skirt. Everything was going according to plan . . . except the applause was only semi-inspired, at best.

At the crowning, I was angry I had to even stand on stage with the other contestants because the whole thing seemed unfair to me. My act was good, I knew that for a fact. It must have been rigged! Some of these bitches must've been handing out hand jobs for the prize money! Which, I mean, no judgment . . . a girl's got to do what a girl's got to do.

Surprise, I didn't win. My ego was shattered, and I stormed off stage. Before I could make it out the door, I was stopped by Fade-Dra Phey, a well-respected art-scene queen in L.A. I'd seen her perform with Squeaky Blonde and Jer Ber Jones, who were part of a collective movement called Tranimal.

"You did good!" she said.

"Yeah, right, I didn't even win."

"You'd be perfect for Tr*nnyshack. Come perform for us!"

"I can't go to San Francisco, I barely had money for the bus fare to come here."

"They do Tr*nnyshack L.A., too. There's a show in a couple weeks. Heklina would love you."

Wasn't this quite the consolation prize! Tr*nnyshack! In Los Angeles! My entire understanding of Drag performance had been shaped by my trip to Tr*nnyshack. Their stage would be the best possible way to showcase myself to L.A. I thanked Fade-Dra profusely, and we exchanged numbers.

When I got home I wrote down the date on my calendar and realized there was one tiny problem: My mother and her new husband, John, had planned a vacation to Los Angeles, and they would be coming to town the night of Tr*nnyshack.

So naturally I decided to invite Mom to Tr*nnyshack. She'd never been to any Drag show before, so it would sort of be throwing her in the deep end, but I wasn't worried about it. I wanted her to see what it was I loved about Drag.

The only distance between Mom and me was the physical distance. I was on the other side of the country from my home, trying to make a career for myself, and she had no idea what that meant. She assumed I was prostituting myself for drugs. And if the vibe at Tr*nnyshack L.A. was anything like its San Fran counterpart, it likely would not disprove that theory.

Tr*nnyshack took place at Fubar, a very small spot on Santa Monica Boulevard, walking distance from where Jeremy and I lived. Fubar was known for stiff drinks and big-dicked strippers. It was already starting to get packed when I walked in, so I told the bartender my mother and stepdad were coming, and he made sure to reserve two barstools for them.

In my head, this was going to be my premiere Drag performance in Los Angeles. I wanted it to be a homecoming celebration. Mom seemed fine, distracted by the husband. He was doing his best to be accepting, although his pasted-on smile conveyed the fact that he had never imagined himself squeezed into a sweaty gay bar, being hit on by terrifying Drag queens. None of them was more terrifying than Heklina herself, the empress of Tr*nnyshack, who checked on them both to make sure they were having a good time and bought my mother a drink.

For my number, I did a lip-sync to "Don't Cry Out Loud" by Melissa

Manchester, an overwrought, cringeworthy camp song that I've always loved. I was mostly naked, in a jock strap and a barely there tube top, with the letters *L* and *A* duct-taped to my stomach. I stood on a box, pretending to be modest, as my backup performer (Jeremy in Lycra) circled around me, hosing me down with cans of spray tan. The front row was gagging, I mean literally gagging on the noxious fumes. Jeremy went through four cans, then removed the duct tape from my body, so *LA* stood out boldly on my pasty skin against my newly orange spray tan. I then took one of the cans to the back wall, sprayed out the letters *A S K A* and stood between them. *LA* suddenly became *ALASKA*.

I don't know if any of this could be considered groundbreaking, but it was a hit. The audience loved me. The DJ announced my mother was in the audience, and they threw a spotlight on her, to great applause. Heklina told me she came down to L.A. to do Tr*nnyshack four times a year, and I was welcome to be one of her regular performers.

Mom said she had a good time, but we didn't talk much about the show afterward. She didn't seem horrified; it was more like I'd been performing in some foreign language, and she didn't understand any of it but was too polite to say so. We said our goodbyes, and I shook the new husband's hand. Then I went out to the after-party to celebrate my successful induction into the world of Hollywood Drag. Whatever this night was, I knew it was a step in the right direction.

TEN

I Love Stevie Nicks

After my Tr*nnyshack debut, the producers of a downtown party event called Shits & Giggles somehow got my phone number.

"We loved you, we want you to do exactly what you did at Tr*nnyshack."

I was feeling quite big in my britches. I had never been *called* to be *asked* to be in a *show* before. I was so in demand! They liked me! They really liked me! This was my big break!

"I would be happy to perform for you," I said. "But no, I don't want to repeat a performance I've already done. I want to do something new."

Typically in show business, you find an act that works, that people like, that gets you bookings. Then you do that act, more people like it, and you get more bookings. It's really not that complicated. Had I had any sense at the time, I would have just shut up and done the act that the promoter wanted.

Artistic integrity was gushing out of me like a gaping head wound. I didn't want people in Hollywood to think I was a one-trick pony. Instead, I wanted to use this opportunity at Shits & Giggles to show the world who I really was: a live vocalist. The promoter reluctantly agreed to let me perform whatever the hell I wanted, and the booking was on.

"It'll be amazing!" I assured him.

Jeremy and I both loved Stevie Nicks. She was our goddess. Our poet, our muse, and the Grand High Witch of our dreams. We would watch her and Fleetwood Mac's 1976 rendition of "Rhiannon" on *The Midnight Special* on a nightly basis. Her primal performance was like an incantation, summoning the spirit of the old Welch witch about whom the song is written. Stevie tore her young voice to shreds by the end of the song, reaching for the heights of her vocal register and casting a haunting spell over the audience and the entire world.

"Rhiannon" was maybe too esoteric for my target audience, but I knew I wanted to sing Stevie Nicks live. I decided on "Edge of Seventeen" because I knew it was more likely to appeal to the masses.

While I sang, Jeremy would play the keyboard along with a backing track (which I stole from YouTube and transposed into my much lower vocal range). As the coup de grâce, I would do a sexy and stunning costume tear-away to reveal the words I LOVE STEVIE emblazoned on my chest.

We went downtown the day of the event to do a sound check. The venue was a large old theater, and the stage was, in fact, not a stage but a balcony box high above the dance floor.

A disgruntled and befuddled tech guy managed to find the necessary cords and plugged us in. The keyboard made noise when we hit the keys, so I quickly moved on to test the microphone.

"Hellooo? Hellooo? Sounds good, thank you!" I said into the mic, and made my way downstairs.

"Wait, you're singing live?" asked the promoter.

The look of worry on a promoter's face after an abysmal (or in this case, nonexistent) sound check is one I've come to know quite well throughout my years as a performer. It is a look of concern. It is a look of horror. It is a look that says, *I think I've made a huge mistake.*

I assured the promoter, and Jeremy, that they had nothing to worry about. Everything would go according to plan, and if it didn't, I'd wing it. I was a professional, working Drag queen. That's what we do!

The time for the performance drew near, and Jeremy and I made our last-minute preparations. Jeremy wrote I LOVE STEVIE on my chest with a black Sharpie, and we wrapped Saran wrap around and around my body, overtop a new white bikini I'd bought from Target just for this occasion.

"Alaska Thunderfuck!" I heard the promoter introduce me over the mic, and Jeremy and I nervously appeared in our balcony box. We probably looked like the two crotchety old men from the Muppets. Still, the mostly full club cheered, and our track started. Or at least I think it started. Had it started? I could just barely make out the driving bass line at the beginning of "Edge of Seventeen," but I couldn't tell how far into the song it was or when we were supposed to come in.

Jeremy and I exchanged nervous glances. I started to sing but struggled to find the right pitch. The low key into which I'd adjusted the track was, it seemed, far too low. But if I tried singing an octave higher, I wouldn't hit the notes. Plus, as we would have discovered if we'd done a proper sound check, the track had an overall distorted type sound. The background vocals sounded like a pack of Druid priests chanting underwater.

Oh well, I thought to myself, knowing that the big reveal would make up for any technical flubs. The instrumental break in the song approached, and it was time for my tear-away. I put the microphone down on the floor, and it squealed and hissed.

I grabbed at the top of my Saran wrap dress and pulled in opposite directions as hard as I could.

This is it! I thought.

But it didn't rip.

I kept pulling and pulling, but, as I found out in that very moment, the tensile strength of Saran wrap is virtually indestructible when layered. It stretched a little, but never ripped. I awkwardly wriggled it down my torso enough to reveal the message written on my chest . . . which was no longer there. The plastic wrapping had activated my sweat glands, and instead of I LOVE STEVIE I revealed nothing but indecipherable gray streaks and smudges.

What a disaster. It was a cursed performance. A cursed night. During the song's long outro, I made a beeline down the stairs. Jeremy was left awkwardly perched at the keyboard as three or four members of the audience politely applauded.

I hid in the dressing room with some of the other Drag queens and attempted to anesthetize myself with the two drink tickets I'd been given for the night. Then, just as I was reconsidering this whole "artist" thing, a raspy-voiced man approached me.

"Alaska! Hi! I'm Bruno from Doron Ofir Casting," he said, shaking my hand energetically. "*We* loved your performance, and *we* think you'd be perfect for a new reality show we're casting. We'd *love* to bring you and Jeremy in for an interview at the office!"

"You're obviously not looking for talent, after what you just witnessed," I said.

"The two of you were perfect, so much fun!"

"Thank you," I responded, tentatively.

"This new show is going to be great. RuPaul is involved," he said closely, as though he were sharing a great secret in this crowded dressing room.

We exchanged information, and I chalked the interaction up to nothing more than empty Hollywood promises, fully expecting to never hear from Bruno ever again.

Perhaps I thought reality television was beneath me. Perhaps I suspected the whole thing was a lie, a farce, a fabrication, and I wanted to keep myself from getting my hopes dashed by a fast-talking Hollywood sharpie.

Whatever the reason, Bruno's casting pitch did not sound to me like a shining beacon from the heavens above. Rather it was something of an annoyance. I wasn't impressed by Bruno, or Hollywood, or the prospect of being on a television show, even if it had RuPaul's name attached to it.

Tr *nnies Are Fierce

Los Angeles didn't feel like an American city. It felt like another planet, and I was some alien from Planet Erie.

I got a job at Fubar, as a door girl for a party called Stallion. I would stand outside on the corner of Santa Monica Boulevard in my crazy naked Drag, holding a clipboard with the VIP list. It was my first real paying Drag job, although it didn't pay that much money. I needed a day job.

Luckily, I was able to procure a dream employment opportunity: working at Circus of Books, a legendary porn store. I thought it would be nonstop excitement, like an MA-rated workplace TV sitcom. At the very least, I thought I'd meet a bunch of sexually open-minded daddy types.

None of that really came to fruition. The store was owned by an old straight married couple who acted like we were selling candles or glassware. "What was that you were looking for, dear? The sequel to *Ass Blasters*? Let me check in the back, I think we have the whole set!"

It was just another job, but at least I was employed. The only real perk was that I got to take home poppers that had damaged labels. I also got free DVD porn rentals, which allowed me to become a connoisseur of the highest-quality male-on-male adult entertainment.

To my great surprise, I did indeed soon hear from this Bruno character, who told me more about the show he was casting, which was to feature RuPaul somehow. As it was explained to me, Bruno was not looking to cast just me; he wanted to cast Jeremy, too. The concept of the show initially was to have Drag queens and their best friends, assistants, and/or partners enter into a contest against one another.

Thus, Jeremy and I found a coinciding day off in our schedule to go pay a visit to Bruno's West Hollywood casting office. We barely had any money, but we scraped together enough cash to call a cab. Traveling in luxury was the only way to get me in the proper headspace for this type of venture.

Being in Drag in daylight is always weird, but in an office environment it is downright uncomfortable. I remember truly feeling like an alien as I walked through Bruno's open–floor plan office in the middle of the day. I was wearing what was becoming my typical Drag: a black bra from Target, a microscopic black panty, fishnet stockings, and faux-fur mukluks over six-inch pleaser heels. Topping off my ensemble were a teased pink wig, a furry black bolero, and a gift bow on top.

My concept was supposed to imply that I was a gift to the casting director. A cocky queen. It was not a gift well received. Confused and befuddled office employees gaped at me from their desks. Even Bruno seemed a little embarrassed, like he accidentally brought me through the front door rather than the rear entrance. Luckily I had giant black sunglasses to hide behind.

Bruno sat Jeremy and me down in a room the size of a broom closet. The camera was two feet directly in front of our faces. Behind us was a backdrop that may have actually once lived in a Sears photo lab. I tried to muster up some kind of pull-it-together attitude, but it was all looking rather grim.

Bruno asked us the typical casting questions:

"Who are you as a Drag queen?"

"Where did you get your Drag name?"

"Describe yourself in three words."

My answer for each question was an embarrassing jumble of starts and stops, followed by blank stares. I completely froze, unable to answer the simplest of questions. I tried turning to Jeremy, hoping for some assistance, but the look on his face was giving me pure dread and panic. This boat was sinking fast, and there would be no survivors.

Jeremy and I left the casting office knowing that we had blown it. I knew how to be Alaska on stage in a nightclub, but just turning *it* on at any given moment, under fluorescent lighting? That was not in my skill set. I didn't even know what *it* was, let alone how to turn *it* on at will.

After a night of hard boozing, the whole sordid affair was never spoken of again. The blow to both our egos would have been too great if we didn't exorcise the trauma from our minds. Living in Hollywood often required such sacrifices.

I wanted to and believed that I could make it as a Drag queen, but it didn't seem like the world was buying what I was trying to sell. Or maybe the world was just waiting for the right queen to come along?

The only queen I saw making a living was Jackie Beat, who ruled over West Hollywood. She was untouchable. Jackie had figured out a way to make a Drag career work, so eventually I decided my best course of action was to follow (a.k.a. steal) all of her career choices. Jackie Beat had a website, and she sold T-shirts, so I got my own website and T-shirts to sell. No one bought them, but I had them.

Jackie Beat promoted and threw her own parties, so I, too, would throw a party. Rock and Roll Drag Bar. This daddy I was dating, Marshall, helped me fund it. I took out a full-page ad in *Odyssey*, the weekly periodical for West Hollywood nightlife.

The first night was kind of okay. It was a middling crowd, but eclectic. Marshall knew someone who knew Alexis Arquette and was able to call in some favors to get her to show up. Alexis was Hollywood royalty and a nightlife star, so this was a major deal. I was excited to meet her, but Alexis wasn't there to be polite, and she made that clear quickly. She was there to do the job and get it over with, which, I mean, I get it.

Marshall and I threw an after-party as well, in a hotel room at the Ramada in West Hollywood. It was basically a sex party. Marshall used to be in porn and we both considered ourselves to be sex positive, but I found out that night that Alaska Thunderfuck has no real place at a sex party. At *all*. Drag is fun for a bar, but at a sex party it's like kryptonite. There's too much artifice: fake hair, fake body, even fake fingers. All these things are the opposite of actually having sex. No one seemed to want a Drag queen around while they were trying to fuck. I left the after-party to Marshall and went home, hoping we'd broken even on expenses.

The second week of Rock and Roll Drag Bar, barely anyone showed up. And someone stole my phone. Maybe Jackie Beat could keep a place packed, but it didn't look like I could.

There was one more idea I had (stolen from Jackie Beat) for how to make this whole Drag thing work: produce my own music.

Not many Drag queens were doing original music, let alone live music. Jackie had been doing it successfully for some time, and there was a queen named Jer Ber Jones who had a big hit electronic song, "Model for Me," which had been featured in a Svedka commercial. A national commercial campaign was a *major* deal in the world of Drag. Jer Ber Jones instantly became one of the most well-known queens in L.A.

I had seen enough Drag shows to know what worked and didn't work. A Drag song has to have clear lyrics and vocals, repetition, and a beat you can hit someone over the head with. Something like this:

There are times
When it seems
That the world simply does not appreciate
Me being me

Well bring up your ears, cruel world
I've got something to say
I haven't always been pretty
I haven't always been nice
But I've always, always, always
Been gay

I wrote that down on a bar napkin and ran home to show it to Jeremy, to see if he could help me come up with some music.

"My field of study is seventeenth- and eighteenth-century music," he said.

"I'm going to call it 'The Gayest Thing You've Ever Seen.'"

"I'm in."

Jeremy got out his keyboard and started putting music to my lyrics. I had an idea of how I wanted it to sound, and Jeremy easily took what I had and filled in the blanks. It was jazzy, like an American musical standard. The whole thing happened naturally. In one night, we completed

"The Gayest Thing You've Ever Seen" and a second number, "The Fisting Song."

Marshall had a friend with a music studio in his house, and Jeremy and I were given free rein to professionally record. We'd get stoned and drunk and fuck around in the studio, trying new things out. I also started stealing music from other songs and looping them so I could record my own songs over it. "Danger" by the Flirts became my first release: "Tr*nnies Are Fierce and They Have Big Guns."

The lyrics just came to me one day while I was at Circus of Books. They flowed out of me, like I was merely transcribing someone else's words:

Tr*nnies are fierce, tr*nnies are fierce
Tr*nnies are fierce and they carry big guns

My music was similar to what Jer Ber Jones was doing: clever, but not jokey. It was humorous, but it was also fierce music you could dance to. Jer Ber had a cabaret night, which was the premier place for Drag queens to perform live music. I reached out on social media to see if I could perform at her show.

Jer Ber was an intimidating queen, famous and also sort of scary. She said she had seen some of the joke videos I'd put on YouTube. "You're one of the queens I was really impressed by," she said. "I think you're funny and I think you're good."

To get words of encouragement from someone like that, a boss-ass bitch, was truly validating. Jer Ber gave me a fifteen-minute set at her cabaret. My first live show!

The cabaret was at Casita Del Campo, a Mexican restaurant with a hallowed Drag theater in the basement. It was my first time doing a Drag show where people were seated in the audience, which I'd never even thought about until I was on stage, looking at these people just sitting there. It was kind of nice though. In a bar, I only ever had a split second to capture someone's attention. But in a theater, they had nowhere else to look but the stage.

Since this was a step up from performing in a bar, I wore nails for the first time. However, having no idea how to properly put them on, I literally lost all but one of them in the time it took me to walk from the dressing room to the stage. It didn't matter. The audience was full and kind.

Singing live made me feel vulnerable in a way I'd never really felt doing Drag. I figured it was a good thing. Jeremy played his keyboard and was able to harmonize off whatever key came out of my mouth. We had been playing music together by ourselves for some time, and now we were doing it in front of people who not only were supportive, they applauded! It was a dream come true.

We sang two songs, "The Gayest Thing You've Ever Seen" and "Believe" by Cher. I didn't know what "good" or "bad" was as far as singing technique, but I knew I was making noise come out of my body that sounded how I wanted it to sound. That to me meant I was doing good. In my mind, the audience loved us. We left the stage feeling victorious.

Jer Ber booked me to perform with her a few more times, including a gig in Palm Springs at the Ace Hotel for Pride. This was a big deal, quite a get and quite a gig. I was able to hitch a ride with another one of the queens, Tammie Brown.

I'd known Tammie from around the scene but had no personal interactions with her up to this point. She came by to pick me up in her Jeep at ten in the morning, and she was already fully decked out in Drag.

"You know we're not performing until at least sunset at the earliest, right?" I said.

"Yes, I know, so what! Get in, Tootsie Loo!"

I was barely even awake yet. *Okay, work,* I thought.

For my performance I wore a one-piece striped swimsuit. I didn't tuck or anything, my bubblegum was just busting out all over the place. Tammie Brown was a far-out kind of queen, but she didn't really understand my aesthetic. Afterward, she said to me, "You know your eyelashes look like commode brushes."

"That's fair," I said.

"Have you ever considered having nice wigs? Or nice clothes?"

The shade! "No, that's not what Drag's about for me," I said, laughing.

"What's Drag about for you?"

"Actually . . . I'm not sure."

"Oh. Okay then." And she danced away.

TWELVE

Step That Pussy Up

Across the street from Circus of Books was another porn store, which has since changed names several times over. I became friends with one of the employees, Nathan. She had it so lucky there; she could put a BACK IN TWENTY sign on the door and go turn trade in the dressing room. No one gave a fuck. My bosses were watching our store like hawks. As they reminded me often, if I was caught reading any of the magazines while working, I would be fired on the spot.

Nathan was sort of interested in Drag, and I happily bestowed upon her the sacred sisterly knowledge. We did a Drag contest together at Here Lounge where I got on her shoulders and rode her like a circus animal while lip-syncing to "Circus" by Britney Spears. I named her Petunia Bonaparte 5000, and in so doing added *5000* to my own name. I liked the way it sounded, like a futuristic refrigerator. It would now be a family name, and I would be, forevermore, a mother.

Petunia and I watched season one of *RuPaul's Drag Race* months and months after it aired, with our faces inches away from my very slow laptop via my even slower internet connection. The glare of the screen—combined with the now infamous season one lighting and filters—made watching it hurt my eyes.

The emotional pain was harder to face. These girls were literally living my dream. There was Tammie Brown and Ongina, both of whom I knew personally. I could be right there with them, if only I hadn't totally blown that casting interview with Bruno.

That fucking casting interview. Just thinking about that day made me want to cry. However, by the time the casting call for season two was announced, my bruised ego had turned me bitter. *I'm not good enough to be on your show, eh? I'll show you.*

On my day off from Circus of Books, I shot a ramshackle audition tape. Through some miracle of method acting, I assumed the character of a desperate, busted, compulsive liar, alcoholic Drag queen who would stoop to any level for her fifteen minutes of fame. There were a series of items the tape was supposed to cover, like "What three words best describe (your Drag character)?"

"*Drug-addicted whore. Bat-shit crazy. Hot-mess city. Just a real cunt.* That's four words."

For my "closet tour," I didn't show a single item of clothing. I mostly just plugged "Tr*nnies Are Fierce." And for my origin story, I stated, "I was born in the wagon of a traveling show."

I put the tape on my fledgling YouTube channel and called it "Alaska Thunderfuck Wants to Be on TV." It was meant to be a middle finger to the casting directors who had overlooked me. I was never even called in for an interview, so it either worked too well or didn't work at all. The whole thing was maybe a little too meta—and messy. I still consider it to be my finest audition tape.

When the cast of season two was announced, I was fully and completely seething with jealousy. Raven and Morgan McMichaels, two of the top queens of West Hollywood, were cast. Immediately after the announcement, both their social media numbers blew up.

Raven and Morgan were both gorgeous girls, glamour girls, with great stage presence. Very much not me. It wasn't hard to look at them, and then look at myself, and see why they'd be cast on television. For the first time I started sincerely reconsidering my Drag style. Maybe I did need to develop more and try something different.

I started exploring glamour and figuring out ways to elevate my aesthetic. I knew what I liked, but my sensibility wasn't coming from an educated place. The history of Drag did not mean much to Alaska, and that needed to change if I wanted to become a world-famous Drag queen. I started learning about great impersonators, like Danny La Rue, Charles Pierce, Craig Russell, and Jim Bailey. They were all professional Drag queens who made a living. Then there was Mother Flawless Sabrina, whose documentary, *The Queen*, was released in 1968. That documentary gave us some of Drag's most well-known phrases. The bravery it took to do Drag at that time was astonishing and inspiring. Drag was dangerous back then . . . not much has changed since.

The more I learned about Drag, the more I loved and appreciated it as an art form. My look was definitely improving; I was more polished and surer of myself as a performer. I was still performing mostly nude, but now it was less about exhibitionism and more about working with sexual tropes and themes.

There were a few bars I could count on to book me for gigs here and there, but my true home was still Tr*nnyshack L.A. It exploded in popularity and even had to move to a newer, bigger venue, called the

Echoplex. But it occurred only once every three months, which meant I had to scrounge around for other jobs.

Party promoters trying to re-create Tr*nnyshack would book me, but that's not how successful parties work. Tr*nnyshack was a magic moment in time, not something that could be duplicated. Most bars in L.A. weren't looking for what I was serving. Even though I'd glammed up my look, I was still not interested in being the most beautiful queen out there. I wanted to be the trashiest, the cheapest, the most disturbing.

I asked Heklina what she thought the difference was between her San Francisco and L.A. installations. She said, "In L.A. people will pretend to eat poop but the poop is corn beef hash. In San Fran people actually eat the poop."

They actually eat the poop. Illuminating.

Each time Heklina came to town I tried to outdo myself. For perhaps my most memorable Tr*nnyshack performance, I chose Whitney Houston's "I Will Always Love You," which was then considered an "overdone" Drag song. No one performed it anymore because everyone had already done it. It was a terrible song selection, which made it perfect for my needs. I wore a yellow plastic dress and came with two sexy boys, each wearing yellow jockstraps and pig masks. At the crescendo of the song, right as the key changes and Whitney really lets it all out, the two guys in pig masks turned around and pissed on me.

Being the ever-considerate performer, I'd put down a tarp to facilitate an easy cleanup. I left the stage dripping wet, to roaring applause. Heklina came up to me afterward and gave me air kisses, beaming over how much my Drag had improved.

"You've become a fully realized Drag queen, right before my eyes," she said. "Highlight of the show!"

That was so gratifying to hear. I wanted to prove myself to Heklina and every other queen in town. Getting pissed on while lip-syncing to Whitney Houston felt like a rite of passage. The point of no return.

THIRTEEN

Burning Man

Jeremy's grad school was starting to get intense, and so was my weed smoking. It was time for us to get our own apartments.

Mine was in Koreatown, and it was infested with cockroaches. Not very nice, but I didn't care. I was saving up for my next *Drag Race* audition tape. Season two was even more popular than season one, and old homegirls like Tammie Brown and Raven were suddenly legitimately famous ladies.

With every remaining dollar I had, I rented a quality camera and hired a director and professional editor. There was no other avenue available to me in Hollywood. No other baskets in which to lay my eggs. I made a promise to myself to keep auditioning for *Drag Race* until I got cast or it went off the air. Whichever happened first.

This time, instead of trying to say "fuck you" to the casting people, I produced a video with everything I thought they were looking for: muted tones, carpeted hallway runway looks, and the deadpan "I'm really nice unless you come for me" interview response.

One of the questions you're supposed to answer for the audition is "What's (your Drag character's) origin story?" For my last tape, I'd recited the lyrics of "Gypsys, Tramps & Thieves" and "Papa Was a Rolling Stone." I thought it was hilarious, but it didn't really tell them anything about me. This time I boasted of my Miss Fish Bowl crown and my memorable performances at Tr*nnyshack.

I sent off the audition tape with high hopes but low expectations— and a *much* lower bank account. Money was always on my mind. Circus of Books barely covered my rent, and now that *Drag Race* was making glamour queens famous, acceptable Drag looks were getting more expensive and Drag gigs for the likes of me were getting harder to find.

Amid all the anxiety, I started drawing an ever-flowing stream of beautiful women created from Bic ballpoint pens and white printer paper. Mostly I'd draw postapocalyptic settings, with grungy characters running around wearing only jockstraps and fanny packs. The same things I'd been drawing since I was a kid.

This guy I was sleeping with, Jay, saw my drawings and asked if I was going to Burning Man.

"No, I've never been," I said.

"That's not Burning Man you're drawing?" Jay went every year. He insisted my dreamworld did actually exist, for one week, out in the desert. "No one wears clothes because it's so hot. You'd really like it," he said.

Of course I'd fucking like it! It sounded awesome. But I couldn't afford such a sought-after ticket, nor could I take that much time off from Circus of Books.

Jay begged me to reconsider. "I'll buy you a ticket if you want to go."

"I guess we could work something out," I said. We weren't even really dating, but I couldn't pass up the chance to go to Burning Man.

We decided that I'd drive down with Jay, stay for a couple of days, then hitchhike home so I could make it back for work. Jay was heading to San Francisco after the festival, so we wouldn't be able to go home together anyway.

"It's such a community feeling, you'll be able to find someone who can take you home, no problem," Jay said.

That seemed perfectly reasonable!

Burning Man takes place in Black Rock City, which I had never previously been to but which really does resemble a postapocalyptic utopia on the moon. It was dusty and dry, gritty and dirty. Jay was right; this place did resemble my drawings, and everyone was running around kind of naked. Just tiny swaths of fabric over their bodies, with nothing covered but faces and eyes on account of the frequent dust storms.

Radical acceptance was the idea behind Burning Man, and I was inspired. There was no money, no obligations, no identity. Sexuality and gender were fluid, and though a lot has changed at the Burn, gender fluidity and an overall sentiment of unity still remain.

The first night there, Jay and I did Molly and rode bikes around the playa. We came across a sales booth, advertising True Mirrors. I'd never heard of them before. Jay told me that when you look in a True Mirror, you see yourself how other people see you, because it is the opposite of your mirror reflection.

I looked in the mirror, and—granted I was rolling tits—I had a moment of spiritual clarity in which I saw myself. It felt like it was the first time in my life I'd ever truly seen myself exactly as I was. I remember thinking, *Wow, I'm so beautiful.*

It was subtle, but this was an important moment in my life. I'd never thought of myself as beautiful before. Here I was, in the desert, high as a kite, staring into some kind of self-revealing shadow box, and what I saw was something that looked like the cartoon warriors I'd been drawing my whole life. I was literally wearing a mini skirt, a fanny pack, and a blonde wig. What I had visualized with my imagination had become reality. Truly for the first time, I thought everything might work out okay for me.

I had planned to stay at the Burn with Jay for only half the week, but getting swept up in the fantasy of the drug-fueled wonderland, I ended up staying the entire seven days. As the party came to an end, I asked Jay what the plan was for getting home.

"You said you were going to hitchhike."

"Right, but that's because I was leaving early," I said.

"I'm not going back to Los Angeles, I'm going to San Francisco."

After a week untethered from the outside world, real life came crashing down hard. I needed to find a ride home.

I made my way to the outskirts of Black Rock City with a sign that said LOS ANGELES. As I soon discovered, most of the people visiting Burning Man had flown in from Reno. There were virtually no cars driving from the middle of Nevada back to Los Angeles. I waited for hours. The sun went down. It started to get cold. Luckily I had my white faux fur coat, but it wouldn't keep me from dying out here. I was rejected by car after car with sympathetic Burning Man responses: "Sorry, man!" "I wish we could help you!" "We're going to San Francisco, bro!"

Finally a beat-up goldenrod van emerged. Two guys were bound for Los Angeles! One of them was also named Justin, which I saw as a fortuitous sign. Justin and his friend said I could ride with them, as long as I didn't mind lying down on all the bags and supplies in the back of the van. That lumpy, uneven surface of coolers, backpacks, and camping supplies looked like heaven to me. I laid as flat as I could, and we set out on our journey.

Within five minutes I was fast asleep, thankful I wasn't lying on the ground. The next thing I remember, someone was yelling at me, "How the hell did you sleep through that?"

I realized the van wasn't moving and quickly came to my full senses. We had pulled to a stop on a dusty road. *Why are we no longer on the freeway?* I did a quick scan for something to protect myself with, something I could use as a weapon. I found nothing.

"The car died," Justin said. "We've been trying to wake you up for ten minutes."

"Oh. Sorry." I smiled.

We got out and pushed the van to a repair shop. It wouldn't open for several hours, so we squatted on the lawn of a public library until the sun came up. Between the three of us we had less than a dollar, so as the town started to wake up, we begged passersby for cash. They must've been pretty scared of us because we earned enough to fix the van pretty quickly.

After driving through the night, we pulled up to my Koreatown apartment building in Los Angeles. We said our goodbyes and that was that. I'd made it home alive.

Right inside the main entryway of my building was a security camera, with a monitor facing outward. I caught a glimpse of myself in it. My faux fur was filthy, my cargo pants were dusty, I was sporting a ragged crop top and fingerless gloves, with a poorly glued-in synthetic weave ponytail on the top of my head.

I still looked like the same person I saw in that True Mirror, but now I wasn't so sure I liked what I saw. Not in this lighting, not in this city. At Burning Man there was a place for me to exist. What place was there for someone like me in Hollywood?

My cell phone had died days ago, so I had several voice messages waiting for me as soon as it was charged. The first was my boss from Circus of Books, letting me know I was fired. Fine. I took that in stride. The next was from the producers of *Drag Race*. I hadn't made the cut.

Inside my apartment, the cockroaches had taken over. I hung my head and cried, overwhelmed by the box of shit my life currently resembled. *This is my life*, I thought. What a mind fuck.

FOURTEEN

Christmas at the Blue Moon

It was almost Christmas, and I was in a rut.

I had no interest in working, at anything. Not a day job, not a night job. All that I cared about was trying to get on unemployment so I could continue not working.

My mom could tell something was wrong. "Come home for Christmas, I'll buy you a ticket. You have no job and no prospects, so you have no reason not to."

How humiliating, but she wasn't wrong. I went home to Erie and spent a few days with her and my siblings, then went to Pittsburgh to see my friends from college.

There had been some changes to the Pittsburgh scene since last time I was in town, most noticeably at the Blue Moon Bar. This dive bar existed on the outskirts of the city, across the street from an old Victorian blue blood cemetery. It was quiet, patronized mostly by an older clientele who were outcasts of the gay scene. The bar was home to what would then have been referred to as cross-dressers: cis, usually straight men, who enjoyed occasionally dressing in women's clothes and having a quiet drink some-place where they could be left alone.

At least, that's the Blue Moon I remembered. Now, it hosted a Sat-urday night Drag show, thrown by none other than Veruca la'Piranha. Under Veruca's devilish embrace, it was developing a reputation as a place for the crusty, super-genderqueer weirdoes, which sounded great to me. I messaged Veruca to tell her I was coming by.

"You want to perform?" she asked.

"I didn't bring any Drag."

"Fucking idiot. The show is Christmas themed. Do you know any Christmas songs?"

"Yes, one." I said.

"'All I Want for Christmas Is You'?"

I felt very basic, but also, yes, I am that bitch. I promised I would make it cute.

Before the show, there was a rehearsal at Veruca's house. As I approached her street on my bike, I could hear Lady Gaga blaring loudly. *The Fame Monster* had just come out. Veruca quickly introduced me to the other girls who would be performing with us: there was Cherri Baum, her buxom and brassy Drag sister; and a loud-mouthed, punk rock Drag monster named Sharon Needles.

Sharon was wearing a tight vintage T-shirt covered in cat hair, with painted-on jeans and Converse All Stars. She had a PBR in one hand and was smoking a Pall Mall with the other. I was immediately infatuated.

She also looked familiar.

"Did you used to go by another name?" I asked.

"Yeah, who the hell are you?"

Now I remembered. Jeremy and I had seen her at 7-Eleven, before I'd ever moved to L.A. This was Nix N. Kutts, the anarchist.

"Alaska lives in L.A., she's just visiting for two weeks," Veruca said.

Sharon's eyes perked up. "Let me get you a beer."

For the rest of the night, Sharon treated me like the most interesting person she'd ever met. She told me about all her past lives, including as Nix N. Kutts ("which is what every Drag queen goes through 'cause we can't afford razors") and how once she met Veruca she became Sharon Needles.

"Where'd that name come from?"

"Oh, that's how straight people get AIDS."

That made me choke on my beer; it was just so awful but so funny. Everything that came out of her mouth was so wrong and twisted.

"Aren't you worried people will take what you say the wrong way?" I asked.

Sharon guffawed. "The only people who should be offended by Drag queens are women. Drag is the most misogynist art form of all time."

She'd somehow managed to skirt answering my question, and I deeply disagreed with her stance on Drag being misogynistic, but still, it was sort of endearing. Sharon talked like she knew what she was talking about, even when she didn't. It was charming. Her undivided attention made me feel special; she ingratiated herself toward me, as though I were some big deal Hollywood queen.

"Do you have a boyfriend?" I asked. The words slipped out before I could stop them from leaping off my tongue. Veruca and Cherri both heard me and looked up.

"No." Sharon smiled and winked. She had me on a hook.

Since I didn't bring any Drag with me, Veruca let me raid her closet. We were the same size! Rummaging through her hoard of wigs, gloves, petticoats, and nonsense, I was like a pig in shit. I found something green and red and pulled out a hot glue gun and some sparkly bits to customize it.

As we rhinestoned our costumes, I told Sharon more about L.A. and how I was about ready to throw in the towel. There was nothing cool about living in Hollywood; I was out there just failing my ass off. I said that to Sharon, and she sneered. "Yeah, but at least you're out there doing it. I'm proud of you!"

Sharon patted me on the shoulder and tousled my hair. I got goose bumps.

We drove over to the bar together, in full Drag, piled into Veruca's Hyundai Sonata. The Blue Moon's tagline had always been "Everyone's Bar," and it truly was. It was a dive bar with cheap drinks, dim lighting, and plastic ashtrays on the tables. On the left was the bar, and across from it was a tiny ramshackle stage. In the middle of this tiny stage was a rather hard-to-miss stripper pole.

"Do you guys actually strip?" I asked Sharon.

"Oh, *God* no," she said. "Not since Cherri banged her teeth out on it. Now we just use it to keep balance when we're drunk on stage."

"I still finished my number," Cherri said. She twirled her natural red hair and sighed as we made our way to the "dressing room," a.k.a. the bar's kitchen. A couple of mirrors were propped on top of a refrigerator, which served as our table. Barbacks came in and out to restock the bar as we got ready, but it didn't bother anyone. When I'm in a dressing room getting ready with other Drag queens, I'm at home with my family.

After being chewed up and spit out by the glamorous world of L.A. nightlife, I was excited to take part in something wild and new. Blue Moon was packed, and all four of us were on top of our game. Before I went on stage, Sharon announced to the crowd that underneath all of my Drag was a "sexy, androgynous, David Bowie–type dude with a huge dick." I didn't realize she saw me that way, but I liked it. I did my Mariah Carey standard with an extra-wide smile, holding on to the stripper pole for balance. It was all right, and the audience was kinder than they needed to be.

In Veruca's car on the way home, Sharon and I sat in the back together again, though this time we were much drunker and looser. Our knees were conspicuously touching. Cherri counted out the cash we'd earned in tips and a payout from the bar.

"You guys actually get paid by the bar?" I said.

"You got paid, too," Cherri said, handing me a wad of small bills.

I started crying, out of nowhere. All three of them started laughing.

"This is more money than I ever made working in Hollywood," I said. Sharon wrapped her hand over mine.

The queers at the Blue Moon didn't know how unique and special their scene was. They were just having a good time. But I knew I had been lucky to share in something very special and very rare. I couldn't help feeling magnetically drawn to the girls, to Pittsburgh, to the Blue Moon, and to Sharon.

FIFTEEN

Don't Cry Out Loud

I was supposed to stay with Mom into the New Year, but I spent most of my time in Pittsburgh carrying on a love affair with Sharon Needles. It was truly a flash-in-the-pan romance. To most people, maybe this was a normal occurrence. But we were two eyebrow-less, skinny Drag queens who fell for one another. It was nothing short of magic.

For all the fronting Sharon put on, she was charmed by the sheer fact that I was so attracted to her. From my vantage point, I couldn't believe everybody else wasn't madly in love with Sharon.

"I'm ugly, garbage, stupid, I don't deserve love," she said to me one night. It made me smile, and it made me love her more.

We'd stay up all night, usually watching interviews on late-night talk shows from the '60s. There was one with Bette Davis, where the host asked the audience if there were any questions for her. A man stood up and said, "Ms. Davis, I have a question for you."

"What, to marry you?" Ms. Davis said.

Sharon and I both started laughing hysterically. It was so silly, the whole thing, but Ms. Davis's campiness hit us in just the same way, and we were connected by some form of electricity.

We didn't tell anyone that we were fucking, but I assumed they knew because I was hanging around so much. Veruca invited me to perform with them again in the New Year's Eve show at the Blue Moon.

Pittsburgh's traditional Drag outlets had rejected Veruca, Cherri, and Sharon, but together they had found a home at the Blue Moon. Together, they were a super group:

Veruca was the Queen Bee, the one who handled business, and the one with her own car. Her style was cutting-edge and avant-garde, her makeup extensive but polished.

Cherri was a cabaret performer, serving sex and realness. She was the body girl, always with her amazing legs out and her gorgeous red hair flowing.

Sharon, of course, was the wild card. The troublemaker.

For our New Year's Eve show, we were all on stage together for the midnight finale number. It was 2009, our song was Prince's "1999," and our looks were Britney-inspired. All of us in blonde wigs. When the clock struck midnight, Veruca screamed out "Happy New Year!" Sharon and I embraced and started passionately kissing, the first time we'd ever kissed in public.

In the midst of this romantic moment, Veruca approached and stuck her tongue into the mix. It was super awkward. She thought it was part of the show.

Afterward, as we got changed in the back, Veruca wanted some answers. "What's the tea, girls?" she said.

"Yeah, we're in love," Sharon said. She was only half serious, but it was the first time those words had come out of her mouth and they hit me hard. I was falling psychotically in love with Sharon Needles.

When it was inevitably time to return to Los Angeles, I left my heart in Pittsburgh.

A couple of months passed by in L.A., and my Koreatown apartment was feeling smaller and somehow more bug-infested than usual. There was no work lined up, and most of my friends were too busy to get stoned and hang out with me. For the first time, I found myself hating the constant sunshine of Southern California and longing for the snowy chill of the East Coast.

Sharon and I did not stay in touch, not in a literal sense. I composed several love songs to her, on a blue children's guitar I bought off a man's back outside my building. The guitar was twenty-five dollars, the songs worth much less. I never dared play any of them for Sharon or anyone else.

Maybe it was presumptuous and impulsive, but I knew I belonged with Sharon, and in Pittsburgh. I met up with Jeremy and told him I was seriously considering moving.

"Are you leaving because you're sick of L.A. or because you're in love?" he asked.

It was a little bit of both. Part of me was very taken with the idea of showing up on Sharon's doorstep and sweeping her off her feet, like some Julia Roberts rom-com fantasy. But I was also really just sick of Hollywood, which had presented me with nothing but failures.

On Valentine's Day, I sent Sharon flowers, along with a handwritten note with sketches of purposefully awful makeup designs. I didn't hear back from her. Maybe she had forgotten about me. I didn't care. I had made up my mind that Sharon and I would be together.

I called Veruca and told her I was planning to move to Pittsburgh and wanted a job performing with her at Blue Moon. She happily offered me the spot.

"Just one thing," I said. "Don't tell Sharon. I want it to be a surprise."

My dear friend Meg from the Pitt theater program had a place in Regent Square, and she offered to let me stay with her. By the end of February, I closed up my affairs, said my goodbyes to my L.A. friends, and bought a one-way ticket to Pittsburgh. True love waited. It didn't occur to me to consult Sharon on the matter.

SIXTEEN

The first night I was back, I bought a used bike and rode to Sharon's house. It was a long-ass ride, thirty minutes down Liberty Avenue in the snow, with neither safety lights nor a helmet. But I didn't care. I found Sharon on her front stoop, smoking a cigarette.

"Oh, hi," she said, as though I lived next door and came over for sugar.

"I just got back to town," I said. "I moved here."

"That's cool," Sharon said, and offered me a smoke.

The news of my arrival didn't seem to matter much to her. We made casual small talk, never discussing the fact that I had moved back with the sole intention of being with her. I didn't even ask if she was seeing anyone. But as I was getting back on my bike to leave, she said, "I got your flowers, by the way."

"Oh really?"

"Yeah, they made me cry."

I rode back to Meg's, beaming and bubbling.

Although we never formally discussed it, Sharon and I started dating, intensely. Almost every night that winter, whether rain or sleet or below-zero temperatures, I rode my bicycle to Sharon's house. We would scrape together whatever money we had and walk around the corner to Howlers to buy a twelve-pack of Pabst Blue Ribbon for seven dollars. By twelve-pack I mean it was a twenty-four-pack sawed in half and taped shut with clear packing tape. We'd then walk down the street and grab red curries from Thai Gourmet, and then to Crazy Mocha, the local Shadyside coffee spot. We'd rent a movie from their eclectic DVD selection housed in the back of the store. Or, if we didn't have enough money, we'd watch something from Sharon's dusty collection of vintage VHS tapes.

Once, early on, I suggested I should pick the movie. I scoured my roommate Meg's vast collection of DVDs. When I got to Sharon's house, I proudly presented the movie *Clue*, which I adore.

"*Clue*?!" she snorted. "That's terrible."

From then on, Sharon always picked the movie.

Sharon seemed to know everything about everything. She had seen every film and was well versed in virtually every sphere of pop culture known to womankind. It's Sharon who is responsible for exposing me to the work of John Waters, as well as essential Drag classics like *Wigstock* and *God Shave the Queen*. She also introduced me to gruesome horror classics like *Creepshow* and *Night of the Demons*. Once we went on a Meryl Streep bender, watching everything from *Death Becomes Her* to *Silkwood* to *The River Wild*. And of course there was *Rent-a-Cop*, the 1987 movie where Burt Reynolds is a private detective assigned to protect a hooker with a heart of gold played by Liza Minnelli. These nightly movie viewings were a large part of my education on the topics of Drag, horror, camp, and pop culture.

One night after a performance at Blue Moon, a tattooed man started hitting on me while Sharon and I were drinking. I flirted back, asking him to flex his muscly bicep. Sharon walked away, clearly pissed. I chased after.

"If we're together, you can't just flirt with random guys," Sharon screamed at me. "If you're not into monogamy, you need to tell me now."

I hadn't thought too much about it. The dating scene in L.A. was never about commitment, or even emotion. Relationships were superficial, everyone always waiting for something better to come along. Just because you were seeing someone often and sleeping together didn't necessarily mean you were *dating*. I had adapted quickly to the L.A. way as a survival method. I didn't want to get hurt or look foolish.

Sharon was the complete opposite, a serial monogamist, strong in her beliefs, as she was about everything. I knew I was in love with Sharon, and I'd do whatever I had to do to be with her.

"Okay, let's be monogamous," I said.

The next day I moved into Sharon's house.

SEVENTEEN

Family Dynasty

Long before I ever came on the scene, Veruca and Sharon's friendship started as a rivalry. They were both young queers who liked to hang out in punk circles. Veruca's crowd was more the club kid kind of punk, while Sharon ran with the more hard-core extremist punks. One night Veruca showed up at a punk party in full Drag, and Sharon was there, also in Drag (or some iteration of almost Drag).

"Oh no, I'm the only Drag queen that hangs out here," Sharon said.

"You're not even in Drag," Veruca retorted.

Sharon had never hung out in gay bars, so she had no idea what actual Drag queens were doing. A retro-style androgyny was more her forte, and she was able to convincingly pull off a resemblance to Janice Dickinson.

"She had two big brown wigs and wore, like, no makeup," Veruca said of Sharon's baby Drag. "I told her, 'You are a queer, you are a faggot, but that doesn't make you a Drag queen. You have to know the rules of Drag before you can break the rules.'"

Sharon knew Veruca was right. She was fascinated by Veruca's makeup. "Do you shave your eyebrows?" Sharon asked.

"No, dummy, I use an Elmer's glue stick."

"That's not a thing!"

Veruca told Sharon the proper way to glue down your eyebrows. Sharon purchased her own stick of Elmer's, went home, and glued down what was left of her brows, and her life was instantly, dramatically changed for the better. The two of them went on a couple of dates, but it was not a love match. Instead, Veruca's bona fide Drag training and Sharon's punk credentials merged into something greater than the two of them separately were ever able to accomplish. Sharon started doing more heightened Drag looks, transforming into a trailer-trash, Pamela Anderson–type of blonde bombshell. Veruca's looks became edgier, grungier, and far more intense. They became best girlfriends, terrorizing the city of Pittsburgh and, occasionally, New York.

Neither Veruca nor Sharon made many friends in the Pittsburgh gay scene, and together they were either literally or metaphorically kicked out of most bars. With Sharon in tow, any gay bar that may have once hosted Veruca wanted nothing to do with her. Still, Veruca was a sought-after Drag mother and would attend pageants to help girls get ready. That's how she met Cherri Baum, a young ultra-femme with a penchant for doing Björk songs for her talent. Cherri's Drag was gothic and sexy; she was a true "spooky queen" before the terminology ever existed. She was also trans, had no Drag family to speak of, and suffered from undiagnosed depression and anxiety. She hid her deeply sensitive soul behind her killer macabre exterior.

Recognizing a fellow outcast, Veruca took Cherri under her wing. Cherri's undeniable artistic eye bolstered Veruca and Sharon's looks, while the former duo's bombastic demeanors emboldened Cherri's chilly confidence. All this newly formed trio needed now was a home.

Veruca called up Blue Moon, the only gay bar that would allow Sharon to enter, and she was able to book a Saturday night gig. Between the three of them, they packed the bar with hipsters and punks on the very first night, ensuring their continued business arrangement with the owners of Blue Moon for the foreseeable future. From that moment on, Blue Moon became the place to be for the artists and weirdos of Pittsburgh. Folks would stand in line for an hour to get into one of their shows. Veruca, Sharon, and Cherri became the unofficial mascots of the outsider culture scene. Not just for queer boys, but for punks, lesbians, and anarchists, too.

They also became a family unit and let me in with open arms. Blue Moon gave me a chance to do the Drag I loved and to do it well. Where once there was no place for Drag like mine outside of San Francisco, there was now an eager audience of adoring bar patrons flinging tip money in my direction.

Saturday nights were our show nights at Blue Moon, and we'd spend the day getting ready at Veruca's. Their triad was already tight, but we settled into a comfortable foursome. I became the host of the show, getting the music ready in the DJ booth, running the lighting system, and introducing each of my sisters onto the stage for her performance. It took the workload off Veruca, who was happy to be able to focus on getting ready and performing and being amazing.

The lighting system was ancient, and no one really knew how to use it. There were basically two settings: full-on grocery store-esque fluorescents or seizure-inducing flashes. Sometimes the lights didn't work at all, which meant we performed in the dark. Maybe that's why Veruca always painted her face clown white.

Veruca's shows were based on a theme, though often a loose one. One night the theme might be "water," for example. We all had to do three numbers, which was two more than I'd ever had to do at any Drag shows previously. It was too much, to learn the lyrics and come up with a concept and storyline for three brand-new songs each week. But Veruca was always supportive of each of our creative artistic expressions, and as long as we did our three numbers, Veruca let us do whatever we wanted and paid us equally.

One of the first weeks I performed with them, I had no idea what to do.

"You can literally do whatever the fuck you want," Veruca said.

That was not the kind of energy I was used to getting. It left me stumped. "Can I do the same number three times?" I asked.

"Why am I repeating myself? You can literally do whatever the fuck you want."

I had the perfect act: my longtime favorite, Melissa Manchester's "Don't Cry Out Loud." Three times in a row.

The first one went over fine; the audience liked it.

The second one, Melissa Manchester reprised, but this time my look was a little more busted. The audience was a little confused, sort of annoyed, but they still clapped when I was done.

The third time, I came out a total wreck. I looked like Lil' Poundcake's broken-down distant cousin. When the song started, the audience went nuts. It took some setting up, but it was all worth it.

On another show night, I once again hadn't figured out what I wanted to do. I was backstage with Veruca, who was waiting for me to pick a song for her to put on.

"I don't know what to do!" I whined.

Then, I saw it: a bottle of hot sauce sitting on the bar.

"Play 'Hot Stuff' on karaoke," I said.

For the next three minutes I walked around the stage holding that bottle of hot sauce, while singing, "I want hot sauce, baby, this evening. Hot sauce, baby!" The audience was dying for it, and Veruca was in disbelief.

"You made more tips than I did," she said as I walked offstage.

"I was just being stupid."

"That's a superpower," she said.

"Can I keep this hot sauce?" I said, walking to the bar with a wink and a kiss.

I was always perceptive of how people responded to different types of Drag I did. Sharon liked to shade me and say I was too concerned with being "relatable." In a way she was right. I thought a lot about the sociology of an audience: how to get them on my side, how to keep them, and how to see a performance through to the end.

While we were getting ready for a show one night, I told the girls that people with thicker eyebrows are perceived as friendlier. It was something I'd learned in Sociology 101 in college.

"So that's why you do a thick eyebrow? You want people to think you're friendly?" Sharon said.

"I want to get jobs, so, yes, I want people to think I'm friendly. I want to work."

"You're like a perfume sample in a magazine. Universal and nice but underneath that you're a fucking machine gun."

I didn't say anything. It was a pointed remark, which was common enough from Sharon. I never wanted to fight in front of Veruca and Cherri. Not while we're getting ready; that was a sacred space for me.

I tried lots of different looks, and I figured out what worked for Alaska. Veruca gave me the freedom to do that. Veruca was supportive; maybe not our mother, but she was the older sister of our group. Even though I had disrupted her dynamic with Sharon, she never tried to make me feel bad about it. In fact, whenever Sharon was in one of her "moods," or just being a total ass, Veruca and I would bond over our mutual desire for Sharon to shut the fuck up.

One weekend, Sharon wanted the three of us to attend a Rainbow Gathering, which despite the misleading name, is not a gay event. It's more of an anarchist camping festival. Tribes of punks build a city in the woods for two months that people from all over come to live in. It's . . . somehow less glamorous than it sounds. The overarching sentiment was very "Love all of humanity, and if you don't, we'll beat the shit out of you."

It was a three-hour drive deep into the middle of the woods to get to the festival. Veruca and I had never been before, but Sharon had been many times. Many, many times. The entire way there, Sharon bombarded us with details about previous Rainbow Gatherings from years back, including gatherings she attended in Colorado, before fleeing DUI charges.

"I'd live there the whole summer, the only Drag queen in the woods. They hated me because I was more punk than any of them."

Sharon kept talking and talking, not letting Veruca or me get a word in. Almost as though it were uncontrollable, Sharon dominated every bit of oxygen with her never-ending story. It was getting rather tedious.

"The two of you know nothing about actual punks," Sharon said. "You just know what you heard on MTV."

"Girl, I can't take much more of this," Veruca said to me.

The feeling was mutual. We were going to be stuck sleeping in a tent in the middle of nowhere as Sharon babbled on incessantly.

We drove up to a makeshift parking lot, just the three of us. "Let's just leave her," Veruca said. I started laughing; it would be kind of funny. Sharon was walking a few steps in front of us, talking and talking. Veruca and I just stopped in our tracks as Sharon continued on, oblivious. Then we scurried into the woods in the opposite direction, giggling like schoolgirls.

About thirty minutes later we realized it was getting dark, and we had no idea where we were. Neither of us had a phone, and we didn't bring flashlights because they were against the rules. Flashlights were considered tools of the police, and they could fuck up the vibe. The sun went down, it was now completely dark, and we were hopelessly lost and scared.

For the next several hours we stumbled through the pitch-black woods. Every now and then we'd come across a punk family and ask them how to get to the gay camp. They tried their best to guide us, but even the most detailed directions were rendered useless in the pitch-blackness of the Pennsylvania wilderness. There seemed to be a good chance we were going to die in these woods.

Eventually we saw signs of a bonfire and headed toward it. Just as the sun was coming up, we found the camp. Sharon saw us almost right away and came up to us, holding a huge bottle of Jack Daniel's and screaming that she'd lost the tent and had nowhere to sleep. We played dumb, as though we had no intention of being separated. A kindly young punk couple let us sleep in their tent for a couple of hours, then we got up and left. The whole trip was rather a bust.

On the way back, Sharon snored loudly in the backseat as Veruca drove and I sat up front. The adrenaline rush from the previous night had us both wide awake.

"Even though we almost died out there, I'd leave Sharon all over again, she was pissing me off," Veruca said.

"Yeah, it was worth it," I said. And I meant it. Sharon was being a total fucking bitch. I loved her anyway. That's what love is, isn't it?

EIGHTEEN

We Are the Misfits

Sharon and I were always together. Our schedules were exactly the same, all the time. Season three of *Drag Race* aired on Monday nights, and for us, it was the part of the week we looked forward to the most. Every Monday we had a viewing party over at Veruca's, and all our friends came. We would smoke cigarettes and drink beers, watching in awe of all the queens' beauty and polish.

The season three queens were gorgeous, untouchable goddesses to Veruca and Sharon, but to me, they were more of the girls I had worked with in L.A. The difference was, girls like Raja were good enough to make the cut, and I was decidedly not good enough. Raja, Manila Luzon, and Yara Sofia were living the Hollywood dream life I had wanted so badly. They seemed so far away, so elevated, so distant from the gritty, grimy Drag of Pittsburgh.

Veruca and Sharon had long ago made a pact that neither of them would ever audition for *Drag Race*. "The only way any of *us* will have real success as Drag queens is if we move to New York," Sharon often said.

We had all toyed with the idea at some point in our lives. New York was the shining beacon on the hill, far off in the distance. But what I didn't know was that Sharon and Veruca had more than talked about it; they had really planned on getting their shit together and moving to New York. They'd even begun saving up money together. Then I showed up in Pittsburgh and inserted myself into the situation, derailing their plans.

Sharon and I talked a lot about New York. I felt very much against it; I was still trying to get my life back on track, because I had really bottomed out in L.A. Moving to another big city was a bad idea to me. If I couldn't make it in L.A., there was no chance I was making it in New York. Besides, we had something great at Blue Moon; why would we want to leave it?

One night we did a show at Brillobox, all dressed as the Misfits, the villainous music group counterpart to Jem and the Holograms. Veruca was Pizzazz, Cherri was Roxy, and I was Stormer. Our photographer friend Caldwell dressed as Jem. Sharon was hungover and wasn't in the mood to go out. It must have been a full moon.

I'd never gone out with the girls without Sharon before. Cherri and I had never been in the same room together without Sharon. Sharon sucks up a lot of energy in a room, so it was fun to get to know the girls on a different wavelength. We performed a couple of Runaways covers, because all the actual Misfits songs were terrible. But we had a good time. After our set we decided to go to another bar, Belvedere's, which was hosting their weekly '80s night. We walked up to the door, and the bouncer asked for our IDs. That did not sit right in my drunken mind. Probably because I'd failed to bring an ID with me.

"You know who the fuck I am," I said, and then I screamed, "My face is my ID, motherfucker!"

When attempting to get into a bar, this line never—*never*—works. They knew who we were, of course; we were regular patrons. But they had to stick to their gig and wouldn't let us in.

"Fine, fuck you. We'll go somewhere else," I said.

We walked a few blocks up the street, to a place called the Castle, still in full Misfits Drag. I was pissed, and all of us were heated. Then, out of nowhere, we heard someone yell out, "Fucking faggots!"

There was this guy, right across the street, with a group of friends. He kept yelling, "faggot" this, "faggot" that.

It really pissed me off; pissed all of us off. In the fictional televised version of my life story, this would be the part where our psychokinesis witch powers developed and we crushed him like a drain bug. In the real-life story, I picked up a big wooden traffic plank and handed it to Veruca.

"Hit him, girl," I said.

Before either of us had time to think about repercussions, Veruca hurled the plank at these motherfuckers. It didn't hit them, it didn't even make it halfway across the street, but it sure got their attention. These bruisers were pissed. Four of them came rumbling toward us. I took Cherri by the hand and ran, the two of us holding each other up.

After a block we turned around and realized they weren't following us. We were alone. Someone was screaming, "Stop! Stop!" We came back around the corner and saw these guys beating the shit out of Veruca.

Cherri and I just stood there. We didn't know what to do. I felt completely helpless.

Luckily our punk friend Eva happened to be walking by and saw what was happening. She took off her shoes and started hitting these guys, pushing them off of Veruca. With Eva's help, we were able to get Veruca off the ground, into her car, and back home.

I got back to Sharon's and woke her up to tell her what had happened.

"Why did you pick a fight with these guys anyway? You were asking for trouble," she said.

"They called us faggots, we had to stand up for ourselves!"

"Oh gosh, someone called you a faggot, how can you even breathe? If you can't take being called a faggot, you shouldn't be dressing like one."

I was furious at Sharon's reaction but didn't want to engage.

The next morning, both of Veruca's eyes were black and swollen. "It's not the first time I've had black eyes," Veruca said. Blood was coming out of her ears. It was horrifying, traumatizing, and I felt incredibly guilty. If I hadn't told her to pick up that plank, none of that would have happened. They were the ones who started it. They were heckling us, and sure, it was just words, but they were heckling us to show they had power over us. They and their toxic masculinity wanted us to feel small, and we weren't going to take that shit.

Maybe Sharon was right. Maybe provoking them was really stupid, but what's the right move in that scenario? Stand up for yourself and risk bodily harm? Or stay quiet and let someone treat you like you're worthless? I don't know the answer, but at the end of the day, it wasn't my body that ended up bloody and bruised, and I felt so ashamed for what happened to Veruca.

A queer visibility and safety rally started the next morning at the site of the attack. "No more queer violence" was our rallying cry. It was a pretty big crowd. A lot of people blackened their eyes with makeup in solidarity. All the news stations in the city were there. They did not like us; they knew we were troublemakers. Sharon showed up in female cop

Drag with a blonde wig and a megaphone, screaming out, "Don't hate us because we're beautiful!"

Veruca was surprised and warmed that the whole city showed up for her. She gave an exceptionally eloquent speech, taking the whole thing in stride. The truly upsetting part to her was that she hadn't been able to fight back. Her shoes were ankle boots with a zipper, so once she went down she wasn't able to get back up and fight. A Drag queen shouldn't have to worry about how her shoes will hold up if she gets jumped. But this was the world we lived in.

Caldwell arranged a photo shoot with Veruca, featuring all of her bruises. The whole look was very much in keeping with her grunge aesthetic, and those photos were featured in an art exhibit at the Warhol Museum. Veruca thought it was cool. Whenever someone would offer her their condolences, Veruca would say, "What do you tell a Drag queen with two black eyes? Nothing, you already told her twice."

Soon after the incident, Veruca grew tired of waiting for Sharon and decided to move to New York by herself.

"Are you scared of getting attacked again?" I asked her.

"I carry two knives in my purse at all times; I'm not scared of shit."

Veruca lived by the motto "To be scared of something is to give it power."

We had a going-away party for her at Blue Moon, but it wasn't a happy night. It was a deep wound for Sharon; they were supposed to go to New York together. Sharon performed "Always Be My Baby" by Mariah Carey and started crying halfway through it. Veruca came out in Statue of Liberty Drag and did "Empire State of Mind" by Jay-Z and Alicia Keys, and she, too, burst into tears on stage.

Then Sharon came out again and performed "My Hair Looks Fierce" by Amanda Lepore, while shaving her head on stage. "Veruca always told me you have to shave your head at least once in this lifetime," Sharon slurred into the microphone.

After her performance Sharon was visibly inebriated and having a hard time standing. She fell asleep crumpled up on the sidewalk in front of the bar.

Neither Sharon nor Veruca said it, but I'm sure both blamed me for their split. Hell, I blamed me, even though I knew it wasn't my fault. It was just easier that way.

NINETEEN

House of Haunt

With Veruca gone, Sharon was having an identity crisis. Sharon was always comfortable being second fiddle to Veruca, but being number one takes a lot of preparation and hard work.

"We're not going to justify ourselves as being secondary," I told her. "We're all stars, all of us."

Sharon rolled her eyes. "What do you know, you've never been through anything. Who'd you ever let break your heart?"

She was lashing out in pain, which she would do when she drank. We both drank. A lot. We always had, but it seemed like since Veruca left, getting drunk was the basis of our relationship.

We started coming up with new ways of doing shows. Doing three new lip-syncs apiece every Saturday was hard work. I had this idea to write out an entire play, record it, and then have us lip-sync to it in person. Sharon and I wrote the first play together: *Golden Girls, Interrupted*. We all played the Golden Girls, except we'd been booked into Shady Pines, and someone was mysteriously killing us one by one.

We wrote the script fast, and it seemed like such a great idea to pre-record it and lip-sync along. But we didn't know the words; it was a whole play, over an hour long. Why I thought we'd be able to learn the whole thing, I don't know. Getting Sharon and Cherri to rehearse for anything and learn lines was not a real option, so when show night finally arrived, we pretty much stood in place and mush-mouthed the words of the scenes until it was time for a musical number. It was still funny, and the audience liked it.

Pre-recording didn't work, but now we were really into doing shows with loose plots. That was more our vibe, and it worked better. We did another show based on the Bible. Cherri was Satan, Sharon was God, and I was a *Mad Max: Fury Road* version of Jesus with a laser blaster.

There had always been a contingency of queers in Pittsburgh who felt that Sharon, and by extension the rest of us, crossed the line in our satiric performances. Sharon loved to push the envelope on what was acceptable discourse. "I am the 9/11 of Drag," she would say. One night she performed the opening number of *Rocky Horror Picture Show*, which in the film is a silhouette of red lips floating on a black screen. With clever lighting and makeup, Sharon was able to pull off the effect in the bar; but once it was over and the lights came back on, Sharon's face was painted black, and her lips bright red.

Was it her intention to give the appearance of blackface? It sure got the attention of a few vocal detractors. Another night, Sharon came out in a Confederate flag bikini, holding a fake gun, performing "Proud to Be an American." No redneck would have thought she was in support of the Confederacy, but it was still a striking and unsettling image on stage in a gay bar.

"We are provocateurs," Sharon told Cherri and me. "We should not only be socially terrifying, we should be anti-Drag, anti-pageant, anti-glamour."

"I don't want an audience to hate us. I want them to have fun," I said.

"Well, the rest of us are trying to be disgusting monsters, but you just continue making it blonde and tan and boring," Sharon said. She seemed to be actively working to destroy any goodwill our artistic endeavors had ever garnered.

To properly convey her role as the new HBIC of Blue Moon, Sharon threw a party called "Night of 1,000 Sharons." We hired a few local queens, all of whom were to appear in Sharon Needles Drag. In an attempt to truly emulate Sharon, I wore the Confederate flag bikini. Not to be outdone by comparisons, Sharon performed wearing Mickey Mouse ears and a Nazi swastika, a total parody of Sharon Needles taken to the extreme. During her performance number, she blurted out the N-word. The bulk of the audience didn't hear what she said. Some appreciated it for its satiric intention, but there were others who were clearly taken aback. I felt embarrassed, for Sharon and for myself.

Surely this was a step too far. In the cramped backstage I screamed at her, "You need to stop this shit. It's not okay, you're hurting people and alienating people and making them uncomfortable in queer spaces."

"It's my job to push buttons. I'm not here to look pretty and be approachable, like you."

"If you want to push buttons, push the buttons that belong to you. Get on stage and get everyone to call you a faggot and spit on you."

"A lot of homos were killed in the Holocaust, you know. And Disney supported Nazis but no one cares. They blindly support commercialism and pop stars."

"You can't say the N-word, Sharon, I don't care how provocative you're trying to be. You just can't do it."

"*Faggot* has two *g*'s in it too, you know."

What a hypocrite I felt like, wearing a motherfucking Confederate flag while claiming moral high ground. Part of me understood Sharon's nature because being perverse was such a deep and visceral aspect of Drag. We are meant to push boundaries; Divine literally picked up a piece of shit and ate it, on camera. This was our history. Sharon thought there was no limit to acceptable comedy, but neither of us really realized at the time how tone-deaf this kind of parody was. This was too far, and I should have tried to stop her. We were white and privileged, and we were allowed to be shocking in ways others weren't.

The community we had created at Blue Moon was one of inclusion and acceptance of all people. How could that continue if we were going to alienate audiences? Cracks were showing, even if I was only beginning to see them.

Sharon didn't come home with me that night; she went out drinking with some of her anarchist friends. She got back late, but I was still up. We both pretended the fight never happened.

"I got us a paying gig for a Halloween party," she said.

"That's great."

"One thing though, we have to pretend we're a band; it's not really a lip-syncing kind of party."

"Well, what's the name of our band?" I asked.

"House of Haunt!"

It was the first time I'd heard the term. The next morning I got the full story. Sharon had been drinking and "innocently" flirting with these anarchists and, amid all her shit talk, had told them she was not only in a band but that all the members of the band were Drag versions of Hollywood monsters. They called her out on her bullshit and told her that if she was telling the truth, she should come perform at their squat house. They'd give her fifty dollars if she actually turned up and performed. Sharon, never one to turn down a dare or a fifty, told them we'd be there.

Now here we were. The birth of the House of Haunt.

The squat house/venue was called Helter Shelter, and it was located directly behind the Allegheny Cemetery. We walked through the grave-yard in costume: Sharon was a glam Dracula, I was sexy Frankenstein, and Cherri was the sultry Creature from the Black Lagoon. We carried 1960s Halloween blow mold figures, which were our stage props. To get to the venue, we jumped over the back fence of the graveyard, blow molds first. Sharon and I hoisted up Cherri, then we each made our way.

"Are we going to be safe in this place?" I asked Sharon.

"What does 'safe' have to do with anything?" she said. "You're so boring, you're like Marilyn on *The Munsters*. Poor thing—she's the pretty prom queen!"

We just kept walking.

None of us had any talent for instrumentation, but that didn't matter. Sharon marketed us as a noise band. We had a soundboard operator who would manipulate sounds we made. Rusty metal pieces rubbing against each other over an echoing microphone. It was a rudimentary setup, but spooky and effective. We each took turns reading trick-or-treating tips off of plastic Halloween bags. Mine was tip number one: "Wear reflective clothing."

We made it out of Helter Shelter alive and fifty dollars richer. The next time I heard the phrase *House of Haunt*, Sharon was saying it on television. The thing is, Sharon was never really that spooky of a queen back then. Cherri was kind of goth, and Veruca too, to an extent. But Sharon Needles was a bimbo blonde—at least, that's how she presented herself. Sharon wanted to be Amanda Lepore, not Elvira, Mistress of the Dark. Really the blondeness was a false front, from behind which she could be insidiously politically incorrect, a hellish provocateur. "When you mix smart and dumb you get a show like no other," she would say.

The following month we had a Thanksgiving-themed show at Blue Moon. It was a big production for us, with a buffet and everything. Sharon planned a show based around food; every number had some sort of actual piece of food incorporated. Cherri did "Cherry Pie" by Warrant, and Sharon did "Milkshake" by Kelis, with two gallons of 2 percent milk, which she poured all over herself (as well as the first two rows).

My number was to "Piece of Me" by Britney Spears. I tore apart a turkey. At the end of the show, we all came back onstage to "Girls Just Want to Have Fun" by Cyndi Lauper. We grabbed all the leftovers from the buffet and had a giant food fight. The bar was destroyed, but it was a good time. I stayed afterward to clean up our mess, which made Sharon furious.

"You're always so nice, it's disturbing. You're like the personification of the Rachel haircut."

"Cleaning up after myself may not be good for street cred, but it ensures our continued employment," I said.

We made our way home, drunk and quiet. I got my key out to open the door and Sharon stopped me.

"Look," she said.

I looked up, and there, spray-painted across the front of our house, in giant letters: RACIST.

It was humiliating and horrifying. My face felt red with fear but also guilt. As scary as it was, I couldn't help but feel we'd brought this on ourselves. Even Sharon was taken aback, slightly. On top of the vandalism, our house had been robbed. I felt like I was having a heart attack, but I later realized it was my first panic attack.

TWENTY

New York

The performance artist Justin Vivian Bond put up a casting call notice online for a new show in New York. It was her first big show since Kiki and Herb. I felt very responsible, getting on a bus from Pittsburgh to New York City to audition for Mx. Bond, a real-life legend of the underground queer community. Sharon came with me, and that night we went out in New York, in Drag, with Veruca. It was so glamorous, like we were celebrities.

The audition went well; I got a really good role. That meant I'd have to move to New York for a month. I brought it up to Sharon, who was immediately resentful, for which I couldn't blame her. After making her stay behind in Pittsburgh, now I would be going to New York anyway? But then, that didn't seem to be what she was really mad about. She was more resentful of the fact that I'd be in New York, surrounded by men. She seemed convinced I was going to cheat on her.

"I'll stay with Veruca," I said. "I won't even be able to cheat if I wanted to."

Sharon begrudgingly agreed to let me go. She came with me to the bus station and saw me to the bus.

"I'll never forgive you for cheating on me," she said.

"I didn't cheat on you."

"Not yet."

I boarded and she waited outside until we took off. I realized then that Sharon and I had pretty much not spent more than an hour apart since we had started dating. Maybe it was good we were spending some time away from each other.

Veruca was living in Bushwick at a queer house called the Castle. I figured out the subways and hid behind thick black sunglasses at all times. New York was intense, and it was fucking hard. I got lost all the time, often heading uptown on an express train when I'd only meant to go to Union Square.

The show was called *Re:Galli Blonde*; it told the story of the Galli, a tribe of genderfluid priests and priestesses who lived outside the city and outside of society in the ancient Mediterranean. Reviews were mixed. Mx. Bond wrote a sweeping, epic story with the intention of educating the audience about this lofty, little-known subject matter. The audience, however, was expecting Kiki and Herb Part Two. But still, I was working with a legend, a respectable achievement on my resume. New York was challenging but exciting. And I felt like I fit in, especially once I got a stronger understanding of the trains.

The last night of the show was a real party. I took ecstasy and made out with a queen who was in Drag. I don't know if that's technically cheating, but it was enough for me to feel guilty in the midst of Sharon's ongoing suspicions.

It didn't help that I somehow got scabies and brought it back to Pittsburgh with me, which meant Sharon also had scabies. We thought it was just dry skin, but when we realized we both had it, we went to a doctor who told us it was definitely scabies. He gave us a cream to put on.

"At least it wasn't gonorrhea, right?" Sharon said it as a joke, but the passive-aggressive "jokes" insinuating I was cheating were becoming constant.

Sharon's birthday was on a Monday that year, so I planned a night at home with her before we'd head off to party with all our friends. I ordered a heart-shaped pizza, two bottles of wine, and even flowers. Everything was going great; we were smoking, chilling, and talking about future plans.

"Let's just do it, let's move to New York," I said. "If I'm a New York queen, the *Drag Race* producers will take me more seriously."

This plan did not make Sharon happy, and it wasn't just because I'd wanted to base my existence around the perceived whims of a television show. Ever since Veruca moved to New York, Sharon had turned on the

Big Apple. I implored her to think more strategically. "I want to pursue this thing with everything I've got, I don't want to just be someone's boyfriend."

This made Sharon furious. She picked up the heart-shaped pizza and threw it across the room. "How appropriate," she said. "You're breaking up with me on my birthday? That's really great."

"That's not what I said." But she wasn't listening. We argued back and forth as I tried to explain to her what I meant, that I *did* want to be with her, that I wanted her in New York with me. It didn't matter.

It started getting late, and we were late for the party. "If you don't want to be my boyfriend, I don't think you should come hang out with us. They're all my friends, not yours. And you probably shouldn't perform at Blue Moon anymore," Sharon said.

That was devastating. She was laying claim to all the new friends I'd made and the success and validation I'd found at Blue Moon. Sharon was my access point to all of it; if she cut me off, I would have no support system.

I started to cry, which made Sharon cry even bigger. She turned away from me, head in her hands, and said, "I just need someone to tell me that everything's going to be okay." I didn't know how to respond; how could I? Nothing seemed okay to me.

Then, through Joan Crawford tears, Sharon pulled herself together.

"Everything's going to be okay," she said, to herself as much as to me. It was all very dramatic, which was our normal. But by then, things started to become clearer to me. This was the Sharon Show, and everyone else was just a secondary character.

After that fight, I dropped New York as an option. I'd truly come to accept that Sharon was in charge, and if I wanted to stay with her, that's how it was going to be. The seduction ran deep; I wanted to be around her and would do what I had to do to ensure she wanted to be around me.

My life was to be all about Sharon and what she wanted. And if I wanted to keep things smooth, I better surrender to that. Sharon owned me. She already knew that, but I had finally caught on to what had been happening right in front of my face.

TWENTY-ONE

Downtown Drag Clowns

Drag Race season four auditions were coming up, and Cherri and I were constantly talking about what we were doing for our audition tapes.

Sharon thought it was ridiculous that we were even bothering to audition. "They don't want anything to do with downtown Drag clowns like us," she'd say, almost like a mantra.

Nothing could stop me from trying, though. Cherri, too.

It was my fourth year auditioning, but only my first since having a steady job. Saturday nights at Blue Moon had been good to me, and during the week I had a crummy coffee shop gig. I invested every dollar I made back into my Drag, with a special focus on new wigs and hair. This year was going to be different. I'd really found my voice in Pittsburgh, and surely the producers would see that. My Drag had improved dramatically. Now I knew what a lace-front wig was. And I was even wearing nails that stayed on during my whole performance!

The audition tape requirements were much simpler back then, but they were still a lot of work. A few days' worth of work, at least. You had to lip-sync a RuPaul song; present a tour of your Drag closet; perform a runway walk down a hallway; and answer interview questions in and out of Drag. Now *Drag Race* audition tapes are way harder. Nowadays you have to present three different Snatch Game characters and construct a garment out of unconventional materials. How easy we had it.

I gathered together my entire Drag inventory and borrowed some of Veruca and Sharon's wigs and clothes. The majority of my tape was filmed in the kitchen, basement, and back driveway of Sharon's house. I filmed my RuPaul lip-sync at a Saturday night Blue Moon show, and the audience of friends and fellow queens cheered as I pulled the microphone off the stand and sung live over Ru's song "The Beginning."

When I had all my footage, I then had to edit it down to the twelve-minute maximum allowance, as per the audition rules. While I was busy editing together my audition tape, I found out Sharon was busy putting together one of her own. I didn't believe it at first. I thought she'd be too lazy to do the necessary work to put an audition tape together.

"I thought you and Veruca made a pact to never audition for *Drag Race*," I said.

"If you're going to try out, I might as well, too."

Whatever pacts Sharon and Veruca had made were apparently canceled upon Veruca's move to New York. Sharon's dear friend Marina was a film major, and together they shot a magnificent tape. Sharon was incandescent in her onscreen interviews, quoting and referencing Warhol, John Waters, and, of course, RuPaul herself. She shot her lip-sync performance in front of a giant stone mausoleum in the cemetery.

I still didn't think Sharon would be able to see it through and actually get the tape done. I mean, I was in love with her, but I wasn't blind to her faults. But she did seem determined, bolstered by my own dreams.

"You have such a tenacious need to be seen," she said to me. It was almost vampiric, the way she was feeding off my ambition and drive.

Sharon and Marina spent many days and nights holed up working in an editing suite at Pittsburgh Filmmakers. In the end, Sharon proved me wrong; she finally submitted her tape, on the night of the deadline.

And then we waited.

Putting together the tape was hard, but the waiting was the hardest part. Weeks passed by. And then months. We spent them working at Blue Moon, under Sharon's direction. We also spent them drinking, heavily.

And just when we had forgotten all about ever auditioning, we were contacted by a World of Wonder casting director named Chanel (no relation to the legendary queen of French fashion, nor to Shannel, the legendary queen of season one of *Drag Race* as well as season one of *All Stars*).

We didn't know what Chanel looked like, but her voice had a rasp that likely came from a combination of smoking cigarettes and speaking loudly in nightclubs. She sounded like a comforting mix between Lindsay Lohan and Juno, the gravelly voiced caseworker from *Beetlejuice*. "Casting loves you guys," Chanel said. "We want to cast you as the first couple to ever compete on *Drag Race*. But it all comes down to the network."

There were several conference calls and Skype interviews with various producers and casting people, so they could see our dynamic together. Any time a 323 area code showed up on either of our phones, we'd panic and scream, "It's TV people!" We must have been entertaining because we were told we made the top one hundred, then the top fifty, then the top twenty and the top fifteen. They seemed really invested in the idea of having a real Drag couple on the show; it seemed like a sure thing. Chanel always called to give us the good news. Sharon would turn on her infectious charm, and the two of them would carry on girl-talk conversations that lasted for hours.

Sharon and I were ready to be famous. It felt *right*, like fate. Fame was the one thing we both believed in with the utmost devotion. Fame would fix everything. No thought was given to what kind of pressure this would put on our relationship. Or how devastatingly damaging it could be to us personally. We wanted to be on television, no matter what.

The day finally came. I can still feel the exact quality of the Pittsburgh summer air. I was working a shift at the coffee shop. Sharon called and told me Chanel wanted her to get on a Skype call, alone.

"You think this is it? Is she calling me, too?"

"I don't know. I'll call you back."

She didn't call back. I was stuck at work for a few hours, pacing, waiting in nervous anticipation. What new information did Sharon find out? I tried calling but couldn't get ahold of her. She wasn't returning my texts or picking up my calls.

Finally, I closed up shop and jumped on my bike, racing directly to our house. On the way, my phone buzzed. I stopped my bike and looked at it. A 323 area code. TV people. I picked it up.

"Hi, is this Justin?" said a male voice on the other end of the phone.

"Yes!" I replied, hopefully.

"This is Jacob calling from World of Wonder . . . Unfortunately, you did not make it on this time . . ."

The world spun around as I stood there on the side of the road, my bike between my legs. We had come so far and gotten so close. Now this? Who the hell was this Jacob, anyway? Chanel couldn't have told me herself?

"You were really close and it didn't work out this time, but we really hope you'll audition again next year."

"Yeah, right! I'm never auditioning for your fucking show again," I retorted.

Jacob laughed. "You'll be back," he said.

I hung up in a rage, mounted my bike, and pedaled as fast as I could. When I got to the house, I ran up the stairs, tears in my eyes. Cherri was there, with one big expression of shock and horror. Sharon was nowhere to be seen.

"I didn't get it," I told her, my voice quivering.

"I know," she said, tentatively.

"What? Sharon got on and I didn't?" I said.

Cherri slowly nodded her head.

I burst into tears and collapsed onto the floor, pounding my fists and cursing the casting agents, the television show, and the entire Hollywood system. Cherri tried to console me, but I was inconsolable. I jumped on my bike and sped off.

I called my friend Meg and, through tears, attempted to explain what had happened.

"Come over," she said.

I went and laid in her arms, sobbing for well over an hour. She stroked my hair, made me a cup of tea, but mostly just listened as I tried to make sense of it all. For years, I had tried to get on *Drag Race*. Sharon had auditioned only once, and she beat me out for it? What was I supposed to do now?

Meg told me I could stay the night, but I couldn't wait any longer. I had to go find Sharon and talk to her face-to-face.

I rode back home, and Sharon was there with Cherri. They both looked as though someone very close had died. On the table was a bottle of whiskey and three glasses. I sat down, and Sharon poured us each a drink.

The rest of that night is totally blank to me, like a page missing from a book. My jealousy was expressing itself as pure anger and bitterness.

Sharon was uncharacteristically quiet, allowing me the full stage for my dramatic breakdown. It was clear that she was devastated; she knew how hurt I was, and she was helpless to do anything about it. Her contrition only made, me feel more humiliated. At least if she yelled back, I'd feel validated.

Whatever was said was left at that table; we slept in the same bed that night. The next morning, I did my best to pull myself together. I was being selfish. This wasn't about what I'd lost; this was about what Sharon had won. I had to put my own ego aside.

"Let's get you ready for *Drag Race*," I said, and devoted myself to doing just that.

Throughout the next two weeks, as Sharon prepared to leave for filming in Los Angeles, our house was tense. The show sent a packet, explaining what she needed to do to get ready. There were certain looks and certain assignments. She was allowed to bring five suitcases, limited to fifty pounds each. Every dime we had between us was spent on Sharon's Drag. I gave her a lot of my clothes, even though she had more than me. A few of my outfits ended up being worn by Sharon on her season, like the black-and-white checkered dress she wore on the runway. The suit she wore in the political debate episode, that was mine. And a bunch of hair. Sharon was more a clothes queen, whereas I had become a hair queen. Several of her wigs were borrowed, with love, from me.

Knowing she would likely have to sew a dress on the show, Cherri taught us both how to make a tube dress, which is quite simple. You basically lie on two pieces of fabric, trace your body, sew them twice down the sides, and cut holes for the head and arms. Sharon used this method a couple of times, including the zombie blood-spitting dress she wore on the first runway, with guest host Elvira. That was an iconic moment.

Sharon left for L.A. physically, but it felt like her spirit still followed me around Pittsburgh. But with both Veruca and Sharon gone, I officially took over the reins of Saturday nights at Blue Moon. I'd already been doing all the grunt work, all the stuff Sharon would never do. But now I started coming up with themes for shows, too.

I hired new queens to perform with Cherri and me, like Amy Vodkahaus, a six-foot-three queen with a thick Eastern European accent and an unbridled love for Cher. She learned to speak English by listening to Alanis Morissette, and she also had a car. Amy fit right in as a replacement for Sharon.

There were rumors around town about why Sharon was gone, and most everyone knew why, but we weren't supposed to say anything. It created some buzz, and new faces started to show up at the bar. Our new crew of queens would do suggestive theme nights, like "Where in the World Is Sharon Needles?" or "Don't Tell Mom, Sharon Needles Is Dead."

The entire time Sharon was gone, I walked around with a pit of anxiety in my stomach. I lost weight because I wasn't eating. She had prepared to go home first; that's really what she expected to happen. But I had no idea how it was going, or when she'd be home. The show's production had strict rules, and any communication with the outside world was forbidden. The closest I got to knowing what was going on was when Madame LaQueer, who sashayed away on the third episode of Sharon's season, Facebook-messaged a friend of ours: "Sharon's doing great." That's all I got.

Six weeks after she left, Sharon called. The show had wrapped filming and they just gave her back her phone. We didn't talk for long, just to make plans for picking her up at the airport, but she sounded different. It makes sense because she was different. She'd kicked ass on the biggest Drag stage in the world and must have known that even if she wasn't going to win, she'd at least gone all the way.

I waited for Sharon's flight, holding WELCOME HOME signs, tears in my eyes. We embraced and it was like made-for-television true love. The moment she got in the car and closed the door, she swore me to secrecy and then told me everything that had happened on set, while I rubbed her sore elbow and massaged her legs. I was so happy to have her back.

On Saturday night, Blue Moon was packed with queers eager to bask in the limelight of their hometown queen. Sharon didn't arrive with me; she waited behind to make her grand entrance. Halfway through our show I took to the stage and confessed my love for Sharon Needles. The DJ began playing Lady Gaga's "You and I." And then, as the first chorus kicked in, the front door flew open, and in walked Sharon Needles, in what was now her classic garb: black dress, black hair, soft paint, spooky white eyes.

The audience went berserk. Sharon just ate it all up. This was her first time being out since filming *Drag Race*; of course she wanted to make a splash. It was like Cher giving the eulogy at Sonny Bono's funeral. It was all about her.

There was an air of confidence around Sharon that did not previously exist. To be clear, Sharon always had the confidence of a rock star, but now she had validation. Her makeup had evolved, because she learned a lot at *Drag Race* from all the other queens, who have their own ways of doing things. She taught the rest of us what she'd learned, like advanced glue-sticking techniques and a new, softer, higher, and thinner eyebrow placement. We all adopted this new way of doing our brows. There was a lot of NYX cosmetics around the house, since they'd given her an entire makeup kit on the show. Suddenly we were all NYX girls.

Blue Moon started to change, now that we had primetime wafting out the door. More new queens started showing up whom we'd never heard of before. Some of them were pageant queens from Shadyside, Pittsburgh's aptly named high-end gay neighborhood. Through forced smiles and feigned enthusiasm, they tried to get a closer look, curious to check out which one of us queer weirdos had managed to steal a spot on *Drag Race*.

As we waited for the show to air, Sharon got a temporary job at a Halloween store. She wasn't looking for permanent work because she knew as soon as the show aired in January, she was going to blow up and be a top Drag queen. As much as I wanted to be happy for her, I couldn't help but feel bitter when I had to get up at 6 a.m. for a shift at the coffee shop.

In December, the promos for *Drag Race* began airing. The cast, including Sharon, were pictured as bionic fem-bots, spinning around on a rotating platform in a futuristic science lab. With her stark black eye makeup and platinum bubble bob hair, it was obvious right away that Sharon was the standout queen.

Watching that promo, I realized that deep down I had still been holding on to anger and resentment toward Sharon over all this. But now that all just seemed ridiculous. A surge of happiness and excitement wafted through me. That's when I truly became Sharon Needles's biggest fan. Sharon was becoming the star she was always meant to be. And I was all fucking in.

TWENTY-TWO

The Crowning

Sharon and I flew out to Los Angeles together to film the finale of *Drag Race*, where they would announce the winner. And, bonus: Makeup guru and then-judge Billy B was hosting an intimate house party for all the season four girls. I wore my white fur coat and a huge gold purse with a Cadillac symbol on it (I'd pulled it off an abandoned car). My hair was long and black and straight. I was playing the trophy wife.

I knew Sharon had made it to the finale, but until that party, I didn't fully understand how well she'd done. Everyone in that room knew, though, and they were all singing Sharon's praises. Sharon handled it perfectly; she was laid-back, self-effacing, professional, and, as always, the life of the party. I remember talking to Mathu Andersen, RuPaul's former makeup artist and creative director, and he couldn't contain his enthusiasm about Sharon. "She doesn't just work with *concepts*; she works with *ideas*," he said.

"Yeah, you're right," I said.

"We've never had such an unexpected pivot," he said, "for an underdog character to turn around and do so well in the competition."

Clearly Sharon had tapped into something big. That was very much the energy of the party. I stepped out back for a bit and met Latrice Royale, who was every bit as sweet and kind as she would later be depicted on the show. I took a little toke on her blunt and made my way back inside.

Michelle Visage was standing by herself. I rushed over to her before anyone else could and said hi. She told me she recognized me from the audition tapes.

"What kind of queen are you?" she asked.

"Some girls are clothes queens, some girls are makeup queens, and some girls are hair queens," I said.

"Yeah, I know about Drag queens, what kind are you?" she said.

I thought it was obvious. "I'm a hair queen." I pointed to my head.

Michelle scrunched her face. "Alaska, you are *not* a hair queen," she said, and excused herself.

So, I got read by Michelle Visage! What an honor! She knew who I was!

At the last minute they asked Sharon to have a gold look to wear at the finale taping, which she didn't have. We went to a Halloween costume store and she bought a beer mug costume, since beer is gold. She wore it at the beginning of the reunion, but for the crowning, she changed into an exquisite Geoffrey Mac custom-made piece, moss green, with hand-placed Swarovski crystals and completed with a Ouija board fascinator. She was mixing the highest and lowest levels of fashion. Serious and stupid. Beautiful and ugly.

I sat in the audience with Sharon's mom during the finale filming. As it drew to a close, they prepared to announce a winner: "The winner of *RuPaul's Drag Race* is . . . Chad Michaels!"

I wasn't upset; I was happy for Chad. He'd done an amazing job, and we knew there was a good chance he was going to win. Chad was given the crown, he did a graceful runway walk, and the audience applauded.

Then, without warning, RuPaul addressed the audience once more: "Okay, I know how all of you are so shady out there and none of you can keep a secret. So we're going to do this again."

They went through the same exact sequence, except this time, RuPaul said, "The winner of *RuPaul's Drag Race* is . . . Phi Phi O'Hara!" The audience clapped again, and Phi Phi got her crown, which fell off her head. Then something fell off her outfit, and she stumbled while walking downstage. At the end of the stage, she raised her arms and her nipples were showing.

The production paused for a moment, to see if they should have Phi Phi do her walk again. "No, it's fine," RuPaul said.

Now, third time's the charm: "The winner of *RuPaul's Drag Race* is . . . Sharon Needles!" This time, people went apeshit. Was that an earthquake? No; it was clear that Sharon was the crowd favorite.

Everything from that point forward was a party. Sharon Needles was legitimately a ridiculously famous person, and I was a famous boyfriend. Clubs all over the world were offering enormous sums of money for appearances, and Sharon wasn't even officially the winner yet! I was even getting offers for bookings, simply due to my proximity to her.

Both of us were booked to watch the finale live in New York, at a two-floor dance club that was filled to capacity. We knew she was going to win; it was obvious from the filming of the reunion and from the way people were reacting online. There was no question. But when RuPaul officially crowned Sharon on television, it was motherfucking 1999, baby. There were thousands of people in the club, screaming out for Sharon.

Wearing a black-and-white zigzag witch hat, Sharon said, through some suspicious-looking tears, "This is not just my crown. This is the crown for anyone who ever got picked on when they were a kid. This is the year of the fucking freak, ladies and gentlemen."

The $100,000 Sharon won wasn't even a thought; it was abstract. Sharon had officially achieved the only thing in the world that mattered: fame. "I don't believe in God, I don't believe in fate, but I believe in fame." A direct quote from Sharon Needles, the most famous Drag queen in the world.

PRIDE
CONGRADULATIONS
ALASKA
ON NEXT SEASON
OF RUPAUL'S
DRAG RACE
CAMEL
GOOD LUCK

TWENTY-THREE

Dreams

Sharon always treated herself like a famous celebrity. I don't know if that was delusional or a manifestation through confidence, but she always believed herself to be a glamorous celebrity. Now that she was actually, newly famous, Sharon Needles was allowed to do whatever the fuck she wanted.

This wasn't like the previous seasons of *Drag Race*. Each year more and more queers tuned in, but it was season four, Sharon's season, when every single gay man with cable, or a friend with cable, was watching. The level of fame was insane. We'd sit at a computer and just watch her Facebook followers multiply nonstop in front of our eyes. Sharon was a phenomenon. There had never been anything like her on television before.

Every single weekend Sharon was booked in at least one city; sometimes Friday and Saturday she'd spend in different time zones. When she was home, she was tired and cranky. Sex was out of the question, so instead we'd get drunk together to keep from fighting. If Sharon wasn't drunk, she'd get mean. She could smell my hunger for what she had, like a rancid meat. "This is my fame, not yours," she'd say. "You should have been belittled and picked on when you were a kid. But you were prom king! Who does that?"

Clear communication was never common for Sharon and me. Which Sharon would I get, the one who loved me or the one who was disgusted by my clear hunger for her fame? I couldn't hide the fact that I was using her success for my own personal gain, which was a bad kind of energy to bring into the relationship. You can't fully be a partner to someone if you're jealous of them, and I wanted what she had for myself.

It was exhausting, trying to figure out how to behave in order to appease her. But it was also sort of exciting. Like being addicted to gambling. You never know what you're going to get; sometimes it's terrible, but sometimes it's so great that you keep playing. Sharon was charismatic and charming, and I'd do anything to make her happy because when she smiled at me, I felt like I was on top of the world. And yet, in the next breath she would undercut me and make me feel like absolute shit.

Manipulation was a common occurrence in our relationship. If I were no longer Sharon Needles's boyfriend, my connection to fame would be cut off. I think she knew that and was letting me know it. This was her fame. Not our fame.

I couldn't think clearly, and so we would just get drunk. Every single night. Without exception. Through all the time we had known each other, there were maybe two nights we didn't get drunk. And now, with the influx of cash came an influx of cocaine. We were too poor to do it before, but now that it was an option, it was a party every night. On coke, everything was heightened, including my ego.

I was so determined to get on *Drag Race*, I wanted to be in Drag as much as possible. If someone wanted me to perform in a show, I said yes, even if there was no pay. I was focusing on my work ethic and getting better at Drag. Now not only was I wearing nails at all times, but I was judging anyone who wasn't wearing nails.

As anyone who watched Sharon's season of *Drag Race* can remember, she did not get along well with castmate Phi Phi O'Hara. One of their ongoing feuds was over Sharon's desire to win a free cruise from the show. Phi Phi accused Sharon of caring only about the cruise, but that wasn't true. *I* was the one who cared about the cruise. I wanted my free cruise!

Sharon did indeed end up winning that cruise through one of the show's sponsors, Al and Chuck Dot Travel. We booked our spots soon after she returned to Pittsburgh.

The cruise turned out to be a lot less glamorous than we expected. It was mostly older straight people and families, with a small contingent of *Drag Race* fans, and Sharon and me. We felt more like party crashers than the life of the party. All the trappings of success and fame were starting to show their tarnish already.

As we sailed around the tropics, Sharon and I debated the next move of my career. I wasn't sure about auditioning now that Sharon had gotten on and won, but Sharon was adamant that I had to.

"They only cast me first to hurt you," she said.

"That's not true, why would they do that?"

"Because your life was boring, you'd never been through anything. That's not good TV. They needed to create a compelling story for you."

Sharon assured me she had insider information indicating that this was exactly what happened. I wasn't sure I believed that, but I decided to audition.

We ended up shooting my entire audition video on the cruise, since we had nothing else to do. This time I wouldn't try to give the producers anything other than my real life, and my real life at this moment in time meant sharing in Sharon's success. This was my life now, so I wanted to show them what was really going on with me and who I was, rather than trying to tailor myself to what I thought they wanted.

The audition process was no different than previous years. I got the call that I was in the top one hundred, then the top fifty and the top twenty. Sharon was sure I had nothing to worry about, but I didn't want to get my hopes up.

Finally, after months of waiting, I got a call from the producers telling me to get in front of a computer camera because they had big news to share with me. This was it. This was my time! I fired up our clunky desktop computer only to receive an ominous message:

FATAL ERROR, the computer screen read. Perfect timing.

I called the producers back and told them a Skype call was out of the question. They agreed to give me the news over the phone, but it had to be done in top secret. So naturally I called over some of my closest friends, and they all sat quietly as I was given the news: After years of auditioning, I would be a contestant on season five of *RuPaul's Drag Race.*

As soon as I hung up the phone, my friends were screaming and toasting and jumping up and down. I got ahold of Sharon, and she didn't seem surprised but was genuinely happy for me.

"Looks like all your dreams are coming true?" she said.

She was right, and yet . . . After all the times I auditioned, I expected to feel ecstatic, or some kind of extreme elation. But all I felt was anxious and preoccupied by all the things I'd have to do to get ready. I knew I should savor this moment; this was surely going to change my life. So why could I only think about all the ways I could fuck it up?

TWENTY-FOUR

On Set

There were only two weeks until I had to leave for Los Angeles to begin taping. The producers sent me a packet of thirteen looks I had to come prepared with and suggested I bring double that number.

Around this time, Veruca moved back to Pittsburgh, worse for wear. Sharon agreed to let her house-sit for us, since I would soon be gone and Sharon spent most of her time on the road. It would be good to have someone around to bring in the mail, keep out squatters, and feed the cat.

This turned out to be a bad idea. Unbeknownst to any of us, Veruca was trying to kick heroin, while also dealing with huge resentment toward Sharon's success, and now mine. Sharon didn't help matters much; she referred to Veruca as her "house-keeper" and routinely reminded Veruca that she was not now, nor had ever been, a member of the House of Haunt.

It was petty to give Veruca a hard time, considering the level of success Sharon was having. But Sharon felt righteous in her pettiness, and there was no convincing her otherwise.

Despite it all, Veruca and Cherri both selflessly stepped up and worked their asses off to ensure I had everything together before I left for *Drag Race*. Both of them were dealing with the harsh reality that two members of their Drag family were going to be famous, but neither showed any outward signs of resentment, for which I'll be eternally grateful. Veruca asked her friend Miles from New York to come to town to sew me a few dresses, including a purple one that got me read for filth by La Toya Jackson. La Toya said I looked like a sad bridesmaid at a wedding she would not want to attend.

Those two weeks of preparation are a blur in my memory. I don't even remember going to the airport to head out to Los Angeles. But once I was on the plane, two very loud girls came in behind me. They were obnoxious and rowdy, causing quite a disturbance. When they came into view, I realized they were fellow queens, in full face. They were legendary Los Angeles queens, Detox and Vicky Vox! They had just come from a gig with Willam, Sharon's season four castmate. The three of them had formed a girl group, DWV, and had a big hit song, "Chow Down (at Chick-fil-A)," a parody of the Wilson Phillips hit "Hold On." I'd known Detox slightly from my time in L.A., and they both knew me as Sharon's boyfriend. I said hi as they passed down the aisle.

"I can guess where you're going," Detox said.

"Same to you."

Once we landed, Detox and I each had a handler from production desperately working to keep us separated from each other. We were not supposed to have any contact at all.

"If you didn't want them to speak, why did you book them on the same flight?" Vicky Vox kept yelling. She sat on one side of the baggage claim with Detox, yelling out to me, "Alaska! We see you! Alaska! Don't look over here, you'll get in trouble!"

Detox's production assistant tried to get Vicky to be quiet, but she refused. "I'm not on the show, I don't have to listen to you guys!" she said, loud enough for me to hear. Vicky may have been willing to stir the pot, but I intended to follow any rules I was given. I didn't want to end up like Willam and get kicked off the show for a technicality. I was going to do this thing right.

My PA got me into a van with my luggage, which was bursting out all over the place. Each bag was supposed to weigh a maximum of fifty pounds, but I was surely over. We drove to a hotel in the San Fernando Valley, where the PA confiscated my phone and left me in my room with a warning: Do not conversate with anyone, for any reason.

For the next couple of days, I was not allowed to leave my room as the rest of production got itself situated. They staggered the arrival of all the contestants because they didn't want any of us to know who else was going to be on. Periodically a PA would come to the door to take my lunch and dinner orders, and several times they came to randomly search through my belongings to make sure I didn't have any sort of contraband. We weren't allowed to have phones, computers, weapons, alcohol, or drugs. I'd snuck alcohol in, but thankfully they didn't find it. I hid it under my wigs. I brought a whole suitcase full of wigs, but only enough liquor to last me three days.

The first day on set was a very long, mind-numbing kind of day.

I had to wake up at three in the morning in order to be ready to go, in full Drag, for a 7 a.m. car pickup. Seeing 7 a.m. at the end of a night of Drag wasn't foreign to me, but this early-ass call time was intense. To keep it simple, I draped a plastic tablecloth around me and stuck a safety pin in it. Maybe it wasn't glamorous, but it was Alaska. The look was really all about face anyway; I planned to enter the workroom wearing a plastic horse mask. Veruca used to read me to filth for my supposed "horse face," and the mask somehow made me feel empowered rather than offended by the imagery. Yeah, I have a horse face, that's who I am. I own it.

A PA drove me to the studio and placed me in an office room, where I sat, for hours, while producers got all the girls situated for our initial work-room walk-ins. They gave me an iPod Mini loaded with all of RuPaul's music and a playlist of all the songs that could potentially be used in a "Lip-Sync for Your Life."

I spent these sequestered hours familiarizing myself with the music. A few of them I already knew quite well: "Free Your Mind" by En Vogue was on there, as well as "Tell It to My Heart" by Taylor Dayne. There were a lot of '80s songs that I love, so even ones I didn't know well I knew by ear and was able to pick up quickly. There were more songs than we could ever possibly lip-sync in twelve episodes, but I learned every single song on the iPod.

When I finally taped my walk-in, with my horse mask and tablecloth, I'm sure the other girls thought I was a mess. But they were all very nice to me. Most of them knew who I was: Sharon's boyfriend.

There was no doubt that people would be comparing me to Sharon. It also felt unlikely to me that I'd end up winning, since the previous winner was someone from my same city, who did a somewhat similar style of Drag to me, who also was my boyfriend. It seemed to me I'd be eliminated fast. I was prepared to leave that very first day, which was a relief. If there was no way I was going to win, I could really just enjoy every moment.

Our very first challenge, a "mini" challenge, was to jump into a water tank for a photo shoot. If you've watched my season, perhaps you remember: I tried to dive down into the water but just couldn't do it.

"I can't do it!" I said, and the cameras show me getting out of the water while a displeased RuPaul looked on.

On camera, that was the end of my water shoot. I'd failed. Actually, RuPaul said, "Do you want to try one more time?" I said, "Okay," got back in the water, got the photo, and completed my mission. They didn't show that part. The more compelling story was to make it look like I just gave up and quit.

After we all got dunked, we met back in the workroom and got out of Drag. I immediately latched on to Detox and Roxxxy Andrews. All three of us smoked, which meant we all took smoke breaks together. I'd known Detox a little, and Detox knew Roxxxy a little from Florida. We envisioned from day one that it would be us three that made it to the end.

As soon as we were out of Drag, we were taken to an alley behind the production studio. They had us dumpster-dive and fight each other over whatever clothes and accessories we could hold on to. Then we had to go back inside and make outfits out of these dumpster looks. Then they sent us out on a double-decker bus to film some bizarre music video for a RuPaul song that barely even got airtime.

I got back to the hotel room after that first day exhausted but also excited. I wasn't nervous, nor did I consider anyone else there a threat. Just sisters and fellow Drag queens. I wasn't paying attention to what anyone was doing except for Detox and Roxxxy. I was trying to survive and stay there for as long as I could.

TWENTY-FIVE

Season Five Highlights

Even though I was sure there was no way I could win, in every single episode I was terrified the axe was coming for me. I wasn't scared of losing. I was scared of missing out on all the fun stuff we got to do. What if I got sent home before Snatch Game? What if I didn't get to perform in the Rusical? I was having so much fun being there. It was the coolest experience, and after all the work it took me to get there, I didn't want it to be cut short.

I don't need to tell you what happened on the set of *Drag Race* season five; if you're reading this book, you have likely seen it for yourself. However, here are some brief thoughts on my memories of being on *Drag Race*:

RUPAUL:

There are people who talk about Ru and say she doesn't care about the contestants or that she's cold. My experience with her was never like that. Even when the cameras were down, she was chatting with the girls and making jokes. Especially during season five, I got the feeling she was just as excited to be there as we were. There was definitely a mutual respect between the contestants and the host. The respect went both ways.

The first queen eliminated. She helped me into my plastic dress for the first challenge. She stapled me into it. I was shocked she went home first. We shot the show promos the day after her elimination, so she had to stick around for them. She was a good sport. She continues to do Drag and is a total class act.

MONICA BEVERLY HILLZ:

Monica came out as a trans woman on the *Drag Race* runway. There seemed to be an unspoken rule that if you were actively transitioning or living your life as a woman, then you wouldn't be cast on *Drag Race*. Or at least it was very unlikely you'd get on. Every single one of us from season five had previously worked with trans Drag queens. We all loved Monica and supported her. The fact she even had to come out was perplexing to me. Arbitrary restrictions like these are not only discriminatory, but they can be dangerous, too. There have been stories of other queens who competed on *Drag Race* who stopped taking their hormones when they got cast. Since then, trailblazers like Peppermint, Kylie Sonique, and Gottmik have broken barriers and brought wider awareness to the fact that trans people are and have always been an essential part of the world of Drag.

BOY DRAG:

I got in trouble on episode three for my Farmer Ed/Peewee Herman boy Drag. I wasn't trying to do anything controversial; as far as I'm concerned, I was in Drag. "You're born naked and the rest is Drag." I didn't understand why they were so shook by it, but at the same time,

I knew I wasn't going to win, so I was throwing the rules out the window and having fun. To me, my character was one of the best in the bunch. And I was wearing eyelashes! RuPaul and Michelle Visage seem to have loosened up about boy Drag in more recent years, and then Shea Coulée set a very high bar for what boy Drag could be with her Flavor Flav Snatch Game, followed by ChelseaBoy's Joe Exotic on *Drag Race Holland*.

ALYSSA EDWARDS AND COCO MONTRESE:

This rivalry was so exhausting. They kept talking about it: "We have a history. We have drama with one another. We'll talk about it later." It felt like a carefully crafted ploy for television drama. It made for good TV, but damn it was a relief when they finally let it all out.

SNATCH GAME:

One of the best episodes to watch but one of the most boring to film. It was so fucking boring. You don't have a live audience. The only person you have to make laugh is RuPaul, which is great, but she's paying attention to only one person at a time. It's like performing in a vacuum. There was no way to know if you were doing well or not. I came in with the vague idea to do Lady Bunny. I'd never done her before, and I didn't prepare. I thought I did a good job, but the judges said my voice didn't sound like Lady Bunny. I disagreed.

LIP-SYNCS:

The most exciting part of the show. They turn the music up so loud in the room, and there's so much energy. Even though we'd only watch the lip-sync performances from behind, it was always clear who was going to stay and who would sashay away. We all knew who the winner would be, every single time.

I sometimes have a tendency to flat-out steal lines from other people. In the case of my perfume commercial, I stole directly from RuPaul herself. "R U ready, for me?" That was an old RuPaul saying from the *Red Hot* era. That might have been the reason why she liked my commercial so much.

JINKX MONSOON:

Jinkx was unassuming because she was nice, and her look was rough around the edges. None of us saw her as a threat, only as a nice person. Once we realized she was an amazingly talented actor and an all-around comedic genius, it was too late to stop her.

Finally, on the last day of filming, it was down to Jinkx, Roxxxy Andrews, and me. We were going home and would have to come back to film the reunion episode, when the winner would be announced. All that had mattered in my life was getting on the show. Then Sharon got on, and all that mattered was getting out of Sharon's shadow and being famous on my own two feet. Then all I wanted was to stick around to the end, so I could participate in as much of the show as I could. But now that winning was within reach, I was so close to having it all.

I got my phone back when filming was over; most everyone who had my number knew where I was and that I wouldn't have my phone. There were only two messages. The first was from Veruca: "Alaska, this is Veruca, I just want you to know I didn't do it."

Okay, whatever that was about.

Next message, from Sharon: "Alaska, bad news. Veruca burnt the house down and the cat's missing. Welcome home, baby."

End of messages.

TWENTY-SIX

The Fire

Sharon picked me up at the airport. We kissed and hugged and smoked cigarettes outside the terminal. "We got a really nice new apartment and a new bed. It will be like a new beginning," she said. It was a traumatic way to come home, but I tried to stay positive.

"Don't you want to know how it went?" I asked her.

"I already know. I know everything."

"Of course you do."

"I know they never put you in the bottom because the producers didn't think you could win a lip-sync."

This shut me up. It was true, that's exactly what happened. I hadn't been in the bottom, though I've since gone on to prove I'm capable of winning a lip-sync or two. How did Sharon know that? I took the statement to be Sharon's way of coyly making it clear that even though I was now a *Drag Race* contestant in my own right, our power dynamic would not be shifting in any way.

The caustic relationship between Sharon and Veruca had intensified in the six weeks I was gone. It became an incessant passive-aggressive battle, with Sharon refusing to call Veruca out for not pulling her weight around the house. Instead she was freezing Veruca out, subtly letting everyone know she was unwelcome and unwanted.

Veruca was desperate for a friend. While she had run of our house, she began hosting parties; she'd go into Blue Moon and shout, "Who wants to come party at Sharon Needles's house?" Sharon would come home to find the place ransacked and trashed. It was the cat disappearing that was the last straw. Sharon was sure it was Veruca's fault, even though Cerrone was an outdoor cat. It didn't matter; Sharon kicked Veruca out of the house.

Who exactly set the house on fire remains unknown. However, Veruca was heard, at a party, loudly exclaiming, "If that bitch Sharon doesn't call me by tomorrow and speak to me like a person, I'll burn her entire house to the ground."

That same night, someone put two logs on our kitchen stove, lit all four burners, drew a big "X" across Sharon's oversized novelty *Drag Race* check, and left. Luckily, no one was hurt, and the fire barely traveled out of the kitchen, but enough damage was done that the house was condemned.

I went to see Veruca, and she looked terrible. Just awful. She was coming off heroin, which I didn't know at the time, but I knew there was something wrong.

"I left New York and now here I am; all my idiot friends I used to drive around Pittsburgh and force people to book are making all this money and I have nothing."

Veruca swore the fire-starter wasn't her, and there's a good chance it wasn't. There were several suspects. Veruca had a calculated timeline to prove it was someone else in our circle of friends. Or it could have been the activists who had vandalized our house previously. Or maybe it was Sharon herself, who wanted to get out of the house and into a new place and needed a reason to do it.

I don't know what happened, and I don't know if I want to know. Even though my season hadn't begun airing yet, I was getting more bookings for gigs around the country, and I did my best to keep busy. There was no way I was getting wrapped up in Sharon and Veruca's drama.

Jinkx Monsoon and I ended up doing a lot of gigs together, and every time she performed, audiences would go nuts. I realized on the road, before the crowning, that Jinkx had won and I had not. I saw it firsthand. It tormented me, knowing I wasn't good enough to win.

A lot of time passed before we shot the finale. It went down the same way Sharon's did; RuPaul announced me as the winner, then Roxxxy, then Jinkx. Just as it was obvious Sharon won her season by the reaction in the room, it was clear that this was Jinkx's moment. Not mine. I wish I could say I wasn't devastated.

The network flew the three of us out to New York for an appearance at the Out Hotel on Forty-Second Street. They set up a livestream so fans could watch us online while we watched the finale ourselves and found out who the winner was. My mom was there, and my brother, but the mood in the room was less than festive. Largely—well, entirely— because of me.

Every time someone said to me, "I know you're going to win!" I had to feign a smile, which was getting more and more noticeably fake as the night went on. I was already sure that Jinkx was winning, and I was sick of talking about it.

My breaking point came when I saw one of the staff members from Logo wearing a TEAM JINKX pin. It seemed wildly unprofessional to me.

"Don't you think you should at least pretend to be unbiased at this point?" I asked, pointedly. He removed the pin and kept himself out of my line of sight for the remainder of the evening.

When they finally announced Jinkx was the winner, which, again, I'd already deduced, I pretty much made the decision to indulge and give in to my prevailing emotions: sadness, misery, and anger. Under normal circumstances I would have gone off to cry by myself and gotten over it. But I had a camera in my face, it was a whole moment, a whole party dedicated to my being a loser, so I just went with it and had a complete meltdown.

Streams of black tears were running down my face. Mom tried to console me: "It doesn't matter, I love and support you no matter what," she said. Of course it was the right thing to say, but I didn't want to hear it. I was being a baby.

After the airing, Jinkx, Roxxxy, and I each had a live show to perform. Jinkx was given her crown, and then we all had to do a number. At the end of my performance I collapsed on stage and had to be carried off, kicking and screaming.

It was a culmination of a lot of feelings—and alcohol—getting the better of me. I knew how ridiculous I was acting; I had an awareness of myself and how stupid I must have looked, but I just continued leaning into it fully. I wasn't putting on an act, but I also wasn't making any attempt to control myself.

The great thing about losing was that everyone immediately wanted to console me with drinks. We ended up having an okay night once I calmed down, from what I am able to remember. The next day I spoke to Jinkx, and she told me that at one point during my tantrum, I stopped crying and looked directly over at her and just winked. And then went right back into it. I don't remember doing that, but it sounds plausible.

Getting famous was supposed to justify my existence. I truly, truly believed fame would fix everything. It dawned on me then that I was never going to achieve a level of success I'd be completely happy with; I'd always be striving for some other way to prove myself. Even if I had won season five of *Drag Race*, it wouldn't have fixed anything.

Fame was awesome, it was a good time, but I was still miserable. I didn't know how to stop myself from feeling that way, except by drinking. And snorting cocaine. I had drugs thrown at me in every city I went to, and I partook in all of it. I was performing drunk and usually high. I did a show on a cruise where I conjured Sharon by using racist and transphobic slurs. In my fucked-up swirl of a mind, I figured if Sharon could get away with it, so could I. It was not okay, and it's one of my greatest regrets.

My life started to get really messy. I needed to slow down, but the only person close enough to help me was Sharon, and she was riding the same roller coaster I was on. We were crisscrossing the country for our careers, sometimes together, sometimes solo, but always wasted.

I called my friend Jeremy back out in Los Angeles. He was working as a teacher's assistant and was very much on an academic trajectory. I told him I needed help. I needed someone I could trust to see me through this alive. He took a leave of absence from his school in order to be my assistant. "My advisor told me an offer to travel the world was too good to pass up," he said.

My next gig was in Miami, and Jeremy met me there. He picked me up at the airport. "Girl, you don't look good," he said.

"I don't feel good, either."

Miami turned out to be a terrible show. The stage was basically a small patio, hanging over an audience that was not feeling me. Not that I could blame them, since there were no lights and an abysmal sound system.

I was pissed. I'd flown all the way down here, I flew an assistant all the way down too, and this was the treatment I got? What the fuck did I look like?

"Doesn't this remind you of that first time we did this together, 'I Love Stevie,' in L.A.?" Jeremy said.

It did, but not in a good way. I'd come so far since then. I was a Ru Girl now! I was literally famous. Why was I performing on a shit stage with no lighting?

There was this guy in the audience, dressed like a panda. He was hard to miss, in a blazer and a speedo, with high boots and a sparkly panda head. I ended up taking him back to my hotel room. It was the first time I ever cheated on Sharon and it was with a panda, and he couldn't even get hard. He was too starstruck and in his head about it.

The next morning the panda was still in my bed when Jeremy tried to wake me up. I screamed at Jeremy, "Get the fuck out of my face; I'll get up when I'm ready."

Jeremy did his best to act surprised, but I don't think he really was. The panda woke up and left quickly, and Jeremy helped me get packed for the next city.

"It wasn't me, it was the demons," I said sheepishly.

Jeremy didn't say anything while he folded up my clothes. When all my stuff was packed, he sat down and said, "If I'm going to help you and we're going to go through this process together, you cannot treat me like that. I don't give a shit who the fuck you think you are. You can't scream at me."

He was right. I was acting just like I always accused Sharon of acting. I apologized, and Jeremy thankfully forgave me, which led me to contemplate my other misdeeds: *I'd just cheated on Sharon.* Coke was heavily involved, and I tried to rationalize my guilt that way. It had a way of making me do things I wouldn't normally do. Which was great at nightclubs, where every audience expected me to do something to shock them. But this was real life.

We went home to Pittsburgh, and Sharon was there. Guilt was eating me up inside like a tapeworm. Sharon had always called me a cheater, and now here I was: a cheater. Neither of us had much to say to the other; we both knew that our days were numbered as far as this relationship was concerned. But I was still too scared to find out what would be left of my life when I was no longer Sharon Needles's boyfriend. To suppress our secret feelings, we drank more and snorted more coke. That way we didn't have to slow down and have the conversation. Sometimes the hardest words to say are "What's really going on here?"

TWENTY-SEVEN

Hello to Berlin

Any Drag queen worth her salt knows to always take every dollar that's handed to you.

Mother Flawless Sabrina, star of *The Queen*, one of New York's legendary Drag mothers, spent her octogenarian years working as a bathroom attendant at Lips in New York. As soon as a patron's biological functions had been expunged, she'd be there, tip cup in hand. "Tip? Tip?" There's very little room for shame in Drag.

Tomorrow is never promised to anyone. *Drag Race* could go the way of any other passing fad, which meant any single gig could be the last one. Sharon and I were overextending and overindulging. How much longer could the party last?

Heklina booked me to host a Stevie Nicks tribute at Tr*nnyshack in San Francisco, which was such a dream come true. She was so happy to see me, like a proud mama, but she pretended not to care. "Now that you're on television I guess I don't have to wait while the piss is mopped up after your performance," she said.

I got booked to perform at G-A-Y, a major club in London. It was my first time in the United Kingdom, in Europe for that matter. Jeremy was coming with me, and since we had a few days open in our schedule after the show, he planned a trip for us to Berlin.

Sharon seemed to take the Berlin trip as a personal offense to her. That I'd spend the few days I had off away from home, and also that I'd dare to go to Berlin without her. I didn't care.

The trip started out rough. I'd gotten used to the upgraded travel arrangements that came with my upgraded performance fees. Jeremy got us cheap train tickets and had me sleeping on the couch of a friend he was fucking. I tried my best to hide my snobbishness regarding the situation and focus on having a good time, but my diva tendencies were seeping out of me. Whiskey helped.

Usually when I was traveling, there was some kind of handler from the bar who would assist me. And those handlers were upfront and generous with illegal substances. But there I was in Berlin, with no connection to anything, and I wanted coke, real bad.

We were sitting outside at a Berlin café when a sexy guy came over and started talking to us. It's like he could smell my desperation. "I have this great coke, you want to try it?" he asked.

I was happy to take a toot and bought some for later. It truly felt like some higher power had heard my cries and delivered me exactly what I was looking for. I felt blessed.

When the time came to partake of the coke, it looked a little off. Granular. *Maybe it just looks that way because I'm so drunk*, I thought, and it was a possibility, for I was indeed terribly drunk. I tasted the coke, and it was sweet. "Fuck!" I screamed. I'd been conned. This man had sold me sugar. Jeremy and I must have looked like total pigeons.

I was furious. *Furious.* A rage came out of me I didn't know was in there. Our host was sleeping and came in to see what was wrong. I rather rudely told him to leave me the fuck alone. Jeremy was livid and had had enough.

"You're whiskey drunk and you're a mess," Jeremy said.

"You have me sleeping on a fucking couch, and on top of that I'm in Berlin and I can't even get drugs. Don't you know who I am?"

As soon as the words came out of my mouth I felt so gross. I had sunk so low, and in my anger I was lashing out at Jeremy. But this somehow made me even angrier; in my delusional mind, it was Jeremy who had caused me to sink this low. I got extremely close up into his physical space. He looked at me with disgust; I'm sure he couldn't believe that I had brought the prospect of physical violence into our friendship.

The next day I woke up hungover and full of shame, which, again, is not a common or useful emotion for a Drag queen. I apologized to Jeremy and our host and booked myself into a hotel room.

"Alaska, I love you and I'm worried about you. Your drinking is out of control," Jeremy said. He was right, and I told him so, but I could comprehend the sentiment on only the most basic of levels. All I could think about was getting to my own private hotel room and getting another bottle of whiskey.

TWENTY-EIGHT

Fame Monster

For the first time since we'd met, Sharon and I wouldn't be doing Halloween together. I was booked for a three-week production of *The Rocky Horror Show* in San Antonio, Texas. I was playing Frank-N-Furter, and starring beside me were Michelle Visage as Magenta and Willam Belli as Riff Raff. Production rented a house that the three of us lived in together. It was the first time I really got to know both of them.

Willam and Sharon had been on the same season of *Drag Race*, so they knew each other very well. However, while we were in Texas, Willam wasn't interested in being friends or socializing; he was there to do a job. He was constantly yelling and scream- ing in the dressing room. We had several fights, but I always backed down. The Willam I lived with in that house is not the same person I know now. She has really changed a lot.

Michelle and Sharon had also become close; they'd done many gigs together over the previous year. Michelle was well aware of the tension in my relationship with Sharon.

Many nights after rehearsal, Michelle and I would stay up late and talk, about life and about Sharon. She reminded me of my friend Alaina from high school, who had also been the Magenta to my Frank-N-Furter. Alaina was now a mother, as was Michelle.

I felt familial with Michelle; it was like being with my mom or my aunt. We'd go to the grocery store together, and to wig stores. At the time I was drinking heavily. I kept a bottle in the dressing room. I was drinking before, during, and after performances, which went against every lesson I had learned about theatrical professionalism. I mean, what the fuck?

"I don't think you've been without a bottle of Maker's Mark in your hand the entire time we've been in Texas," Michelle said to me. She didn't directly challenge my drinking, but she was letting me know she was aware.

The whole gay world seemed to have opinions on Sharon and me, but Michelle was the only one who seemed to get exactly what was going on. She adored Sharon, but—there was always a *but*—she also saw exactly what was going on in our relationship, more than Sharon or I did. "You're putting Sharon up on this pedestal, and you're getting it so wrong. There are things in you that are more brilliant than you realize."

During the final week of the production, Sharon surprised me and showed up. It was a sweet and romantic gesture, but it was still only a gesture. She came backstage to the dressing room, and everything she said to me felt like a veiled read or backhanded compliment. And so we fought, in front of Michelle, and Willam, and the rest of the cast. Everyone.

After the show, Sharon came back to my room with me and we got drunk and high, discussing our relationship and how strange it was to have the world be a part of it. The guilt I felt over cheating on her with that panda in Miami was bubbling under the surface. I couldn't keep these secrets anymore. I had to tell her everything I did and everything that happened.

So I did. I just laid it all out. I told her about the panda and one other instance . . . someone we both knew from Pittsburgh, who also did Drag, who I'd cheated on Sharon with in our own bed. So fucking tacky. I can't believe I did that.

It was stupid, but I didn't think we needed to break up over this. From my perspective this didn't have to be a big deal. Gay relationships are often open. We'd been together for four years, we'd been through so much, from poverty to *Drag Race*, and now our love was a public phenomenon. Radical honesty could make our relationship stronger, I thought. Now that it was out in the open we could move on. That was foolish of me.

"What the fuck?" Sharon said. She acted upset, shocked even, though I have a feeling she already knew. She called our friend in Pittsburgh and let them know she knew we'd slept together and that she was fucking furious about it, insinuating that she'd ruin their life and their career.

I was sitting in a chair during this whole big display on the phone. I don't even know if the person was on the line or if this was a psychological game Sharon was playing to make me feel like shit. She put the phone down and continued her monologue of devastation and anger, to which there seemed to be no end. Finally, I had enough. "Okay, I'm leaving, you're not communicating about it, you're just making me feel like shit," I said, and I picked up my bag and walked outside.

As I waited for a car, Sharon ran out, screaming, "No! You can't leave, just come lie in bed with me."

I acquiesced. We drank the rest of our booze and snorted the last of the coke. Then we lay down and Sharon spooned me all night. It was the worst night of sleep I've ever had.

The next morning Sharon left for the airport, and I got ready for our last show. I met up with Michelle for lunch, and immediately she could tell I was hung over and still technically wasted.

As I picked at an omelet and guzzled coffee, Michelle asked how things went with Sharon.

"Not great."

"Can I give you some advice?" she said.

"Sure."

"If you get a reputation for doing drugs and drinking, you won't have longevity as a performer. Partying can't be the main event. Being a train wreck is not the way to build the groundwork for success. What you're doing is going to ruin your creativity."

I heard what she was saying, loud and clear. She didn't explicitly say anything about Sharon, but I knew I needed to make a change and that was not going to happen as long as Sharon and I were together.

I came back home to Pittsburgh, the first time I was there in months. Sharon was also home. We got a bag of coke and a bottle of Maker's Mark

and were listening to Lady Gaga's *The Fame Monster* on vinyl. It was one of those kinds of nights, and we were both wasted. Then Sharon started to come at me.

First it was little snide comments here and there. About my cheating, about my level of fame compared to hers, about my Drag. And then she dropped the bomb: "I found someone who actually loves me for me and actually makes me happy."

Record scratch; I literally stopped the record player. What the fuck did she just say?

Apparently, Sharon had met someone in Salem, Massachusetts, who was doing some sort of prosthetic work for her. They had fallen in love.

"You're telling me that the whole time you were making me feel like shit in Texas, you had a secret affair with someone you were in love with?"

"I cheated on you with models, you cheated on me with normal people and that's gross."

So it wasn't just this one guy; Sharon was admitting to cheating on me with *models*, plural? We were screaming at each other, in each other's faces. I was not going to hit her, not first, but I was hoping she'd hit me so I could hit her back. Then she did. She pushed me. I don't know if I punched her or grabbed her or what, but I knocked her to the ground, and on the way down she hit her head on our thick, glass coffee table. Blood started gushing out of her head. It was everywhere. She had a cut on her head that would require stitches and leave a scar she proudly displays to this day. I was horrified at myself; I grabbed a bag of my things and my dirty white fur coat and ran outside.

I checked into a hotel down the street. I had no money, so I told the man at the front desk, "My name is Alaska Thunderfuck, I don't have any money, but if you can give me a room, I'll pay you back." I was a mess and my coat was covered in blood. But I was well known enough around town, so I was able to get a room.

I stayed in that hotel for a few days while I figured out what to do. Our relationship was over; we'd gone way past the point of no return. There was no question about that. But I had known myself only through the lens of being Sharon's partner and Sharon's support system. I didn't know who I was or what I wanted or what I was doing. My confidence was so fucked, deeply undermined, and nonexistent. *Drag Race* had come and gone, and now with the breakup, surely everyone would side with Sharon, which meant I'd be portrayed as the villain.

This was the lowest point of my life. I felt betrayed, not just by Sharon, but by all of my friends who were also her friends. It seemed to me that everyone knew Sharon had moved on, and no one had bothered to tell me. I was embarrassed and ashamed. The only thing that could take away the pain was a bottle of whiskey, which I clung to like a baby.

My warped mental state began to manifest itself as a physical illness. I had a severe throat infection and was skinnier than ever. Every part of me felt weak. My life and my body were in shambles; I needed to figure shit out, and I needed clarity. Our relationship and our drinking had been so intertwined, so I decided that since I was single, I should stop drinking. Getting sober felt necessary in order to emancipate myself from the whole scenario.

TWENTY-NINE

Anus-Thing Is Possible

Now that I was officially single, several people let me know they were aware of Sharon's infidelities. Jeremy told me he'd known for some time. Sharon and I had mixed up our makeup bags one day, and he had to fly down to Fort Lauderdale to exchange them back. When he met up with her in her hotel room, there was a naked guy in her bed.

"She told me if I said anything, she'd ruin my life and have me killed," Jeremy said.

"She says that to everyone."

I wanted a completely new start and decided to leave Pittsburgh behind and move back to Los Angeles.

"Are you moving to L.A. for your career or to get away from Sharon?" Jeremy asked.

"Didn't you pose this same question when I left L.A.?"

"Yeah, and you didn't know the answer then, either."

I rented a truck and went by Sharon's to pick up my things. Once I was there I realized nothing in the house was mine. The truck was way too big and my belongings could have fit into a compact car. It was a sad realization, but I refused to let it get me down. I was starting over completely; I could get new stuff.

Back in L.A., I got into a nice groove with my work. I had never done Drag without being drunk. Being sober allowed me to fall in love with Drag all over again. When I started doing Drag, you had to be the baddest bitch in the world to make a living. Now there were so many opportunities presenting themselves, and without booze and drugs weighing me down, I was able to more clearly see a future for myself.

As a bona fide famous person, I now had a manager booking me on nonstop gigs and encouraging me to put out an album. It scared me a little because it was a big undertaking and cost a shit ton of money to do, but I wanted to create music that was mine. My job now was to go around the world and perform, so I needed my own music to fulfill that function.

Anus became my first album. I co-wrote a bunch of songs, all based on my ideas. The great thing about doing music right after *Drag Race* was that more people were there to listen to it. The music was well received; I landed at #3 on the *Billboard* Dance/Electronic charts, and "Your Makeup Is Terrible" became a hit. We had a great time making it, and I'm very proud of that album. I worked hard on it.

In keeping with the first music I had ever produced, I borrowed heavily from other sources when writing the songs for *Anus*. The word *hieeee*, which became my catchphrase and the name of the first track on the album, I stole from Isis Mirage and Coco Ferosha, two queens who did reviews of *Drag Race*. Sharon and I used to watch to see what they had to say about her. They started every episode with "Hieeee" and ended with "Byeeee." However, technically, they borrowed *hieeee* from Ongina, who officially coined it on season one of *Drag Race*. Such is the way of Drag language.

"My name's Alaska, what's yours?" That's stolen from a famous Gypsy Rose Lee line in the musical *Gypsy*. I used an inversion of the line, "My name's yours, what's Alaska?" in "Hieeee," and you may have noticed it's the title of this book.

"I don't know about you, Miss Kitty, but I'm feeling so much yummier" is a Catwoman line, and I used it in "Your Makeup Is Terrible."

There were other things I stole. The name Lil' Poundcake was from a *Saturday Night Live* sketch. It was about a doll that gave HPV vaccinations. I called her a "straight up motherfucking dick pig" on *Drag Race*, which is a line I'm pretty sure I stole from Sharon, who I'm pretty sure stole it from Jackie Beat.

My song "Nails" features the phrase *If you're not wearing nails, you're not doing Drag.* That came from Akasha Lestat, this queen in Pittsburgh who once cornered me in a dressing room and said, "If you're not doing pageants, you're not doing Drag." She was dead serious when she said it.

From "Nails":

Shape and file, like you're Selina Kyle
Reflect your style, just keep it versatile
Spit and polish, conquer and demolish
Amaze and then astonish, now drink like alcoholics
If you're not wearing nails
You're not doing Drag

Through all this, I was touring with the *Drag Race* girls, and often with Sharon. I had to go through a period of being pissed off at her for a while. I was mad and embarrassed, and I had no interest in kiki-ing or being friends. She tried to be cordial, as she'd prefer to keep things friendly rather than shady, but I did my best to ignore her.

There was not going to be a world in which people would pick sides. We would be working together and seeing each other whether I wanted to or not. Once I realized this, it helped me get over the whole thing much faster.

We never had any meaningful conversations; that wasn't ever really our thing. But gradually Sharon and I became friends again, and then eventually, we became very good friends. It's too much work to stay mad. Through all the horror of our very public relationship, at least I came out of it with a very good friend.

THIRTY

By the time *Drag Race All Stars* season two came around, I was in a good place. I was working a lot, making some dollars, and I was in a serious relationship for the first time since Sharon. *Drag Race* continued and was getting bigger and bigger every year, which meant my career kept on going.

There was a lot of anticipation that if a second season of *All Stars* did happen, I would be on it and I would do well. That seemed to be the general consensus among the fans and people in the *Drag Race* world.

I had gone through a long period of not drinking, but I never lived a truly sober life. I never went to an AA meeting or anything like that. Now, I was drinking again, but it was nothing like before. I still had some guilt around it, though. Michelle Visage said in the last passage of her book that she was so proud she had helped me get sober. She did help me; if it wasn't for her, I don't know if I would've gotten through some very dark times.

But now I was in a better place, and I was able to drink responsibly. Did I need to sneak my drinking while on set? If Michelle found out I wasn't completely sober, would it work against me on the show? All this was going through my head when we started filming.

The entire *All Stars* experience ended up being traumatic. Unlike season five, I went into *All Stars* feeling sure that it was mine to win. That tension and that drive to succeed put me in a whole different headspace during filming. I didn't want to be everyone's good Judy like before; I wanted to go in like a shark and win this thing. I didn't care what the other girls thought of me. My own mental noise was consumed by how I would be perceived on the show by my fans and by RuPaul. This meant I wasn't able to enjoy the experience as much as I did filming season five, and I also didn't come out of it close with any of my sisters, which kind of sucks.

Perhaps the worst part of *All Stars* was when they had us make over a family member. My mom came, and I was so beyond happy to see her, but it didn't go well. The judges were criticizing not just me; they were criticizing my mother, which felt uncomfortably personal. It was all by design. The producers built me up that whole episode, with win after astounding win. Then that fateful runway was the big takedown, so they could see if I'd crumble on stage and give them the reality television fodder they were so hungry for.

Part of going through this process of self-reflection is not to make excuses. That monster you saw me become on camera, yes, that is a part of me and something I live with every single day. I'd built up enough armor on camera and in the public eye to understand that this was a television show and the producers were doing their jobs. Mom felt victimized by the whole thing. She's emotional, just like me, and she was pissed, too. "That fucking Michelle Visage is such a bitch," she said. She took it personally. I didn't like it at all. It felt gross.

The good thing about having Mom on set was that it reminded me of when I was a kid and I would watch her get ready to go out. Most of her time back then was spent on hair. Girl, we got crazy hair in our family. There was a lot of hair spraying, it had to dry for a while, she wrapped it in a towel, and then there was blow-drying and more setting and styling products. Mom's hair routine was the only time she had to herself. I'd sit on the edge of the tub and watch. Now for the first time, Mom was sitting with me as I got us both ready for the runway. I'd always felt that getting ready with my fellow queens was a sacred time, and now I realized where that feeling came from.

Shortly after the show started to air, I broke up with the guy I was dating. He did not take it well. He proceeded to go online in order to make public every secret detail I had told him about what happened while I was on set filming.

Everyone on the *Drag Race* message boards was talking about it. It was like the WikiLeaks of *Drag Race*, and I was technically responsible. I was humiliated and felt completely helpless and betrayed, which is exactly what he wanted. There was a good chance the producers were going to penalize me for it, and it would not have shocked me if they disqualified me from winning the show because of it. I was devastated because unlike my season five appearance, the whole time I was filming *All Stars* I felt I really had a shot at winning.

The whole situation was bad. Really bad. Our show producers forbid me from speaking publicly about it until after the season was over.

When I was announced the winner of *All Stars*, it was a bittersweet moment. The relationship I had with my fans had been strong, but now my cutthroat actions and emotional outbursts had alienated me from everybody. I had achieved everything I ever wanted. But the feeling of achievement and happiness was so brief, followed by an overwhelming feeling of it never being enough. I'm not good enough, rich enough, famous enough; I don't have enough followers, don't get enough likes, don't get treated like other famous people get treated. I need more. That was my greatest demon: compare and despair. I thought there'd be some point, some plateau, where I'd be magically satisfied and happy. It never came.

I did at least get some closure on the situation with my ex. Once I was back from filming and waiting for the show to air, I started working on new music, which is what Ru Girls do now. It became my second full-length album: *Poundcake*. The biggest song on the album was called "The T," where I finally got to voice my frustration at what my ex had done to me. I talked about that, about having a tantrum on national television, about cheating on Sharon in Miami, how sorry I was, and how caring that much about winning was silly because winning doesn't really matter.

From "The T (feat. Adore Delano)":

This psycho ex got heavy-handed
Tried to Death Star my whole fucking planet
Talking shit, dropping names,
Screen capping, playing games
I've had it officially
The bitch tried to really really come for me
He crossed me like the River Styx
But the sex was good because I like small dicks.

To this day "The T" is my most-streamed song. I don't perform it anymore because it's about shit that's in the past, but it's one of my favorite songs I've ever recorded. It was the most honest piece of me I've put into a song, and we made a great music video.

There are a lot of other fun songs on *Poundcake*, too. I love "STUN," on which I got to perform with Gia Gunn. I was supposed to do another track with Alyssa Edwards, but she never showed up, so I had to call in the OG professional: Jackie Beat. At the last minute we came up with "I Invented That," a song about how the new crop of Drag queens who've grown up with *Drag Race* have queens like Jackie to thank for all the things they love about Drag.

Working in the studio with Jackie Beat felt like a full-circle kind of moment. I had once modeled my entire career around trying to come for her job, and now we were making music together. *Drag Race* truly changed the world of Drag as we know it, but we have legendary queens like Jackie Beat to thank for laying the groundwork. As Jackie often says, "You know why my feet hurt? From paving the way for you fuck-ing bitches!"

THIRTY-ONE

Lady Gaga has always created magical moments in my life. Most of them have been the universe using Gaga to give me subliminal forms of empowerment, but some have also been quite intentional instances of love and light.

Way back when Sharon and I were poor in Pittsburgh, the Monster Ball came to town. Since we had no money to actually attend, Sharon had the idea for us to dress up like Lady Gaga, go down to the line in front of the concert, and charge people money to take their picture with us. I wrapped a black t-shirt around my head like a "Just Dance" hood, and we rode our bikes down there, in full Drag.

People in line were really into it. We made like sixty dollars, which was pretty great since we had no money. Then this guy came up to us and said, "Hey, my name is Terry, I'm Lady Gaga's photographer. Can I take a picture of you both?"

I didn't believe at all that this was Lady Gaga's photographer, but I said, "Sure, why not?" We took a couple of pictures and I said, half jokingly, "If you're Lady Gaga's photographer, why don't you get us tickets for the show?"

"I'll be right back," he said.

Well, it turns out this man was Terry fucking Richardson, who was very much Lady Gaga's personal photographer. He got us tickets, and we went in and we got to see the show. From the moment the show opened with "Dance in the Dark," Sharon and I burst into tears and didn't stop crying the whole concert.

The Monster Ball tour had a narrative plot that centered around these rough kids who can't find their way to the Monster Ball. But then, by believing in themselves and dancing ecstatically, they find their way there. It was literally the story of our fucking lives and was one of the greatest nights of our life. People were buying us drinks all night, plus we'd made sixty bucks.

That was my first magic moment created by Lady Gaga. Fast-forward multiple years later, after my season of *All Stars* aired on television. The show's production company, World of Wonder, called to tell me they had been contacted by Lady Gaga's team. They were promoting her new album, *Joanne*, and wanted me to do a sort of tutorial explaining Gaga's new look for the *Joanne* era.

Now, I'm not saying that World of Wonder has ever massaged the truth of circumstances revolving around events and video footage, but I wasn't 100 percent sold on there actually being a Lady Gaga publicity team looking to me for material. However, I went down to World of Wonder's studio and shot the tutorial in their basement. Step one was to "take a rubber band, which I just had lying around my house. No-fuss ponytail! If you don't have a ponytail, you can buy one at the store."

My catchphrase for the tutorial was *I'm just a regular girl*. It was Gaga's era of being stripped down to, well, a regular girl. She was wearing really short jean shorts and a high crop top with her boobs hanging out underneath and a blonde ponytail, *always* the blonde ponytail.

After we were done shooting, I said to the World of Wonder producer, "If Lady Gaga's team really wanted me to do this, why don't you ask them if I can go see her Dive Bar show?"

Gaga's Dive Bar tour was taking place in a series of small venues with no promotion. They were intimate shows that were known about only by word of mouth. There was no way to find out where they were or how to get tickets unless you knew someone.

A few days passed and World of Wonder called me again. They were instructed to tell me there was a Los Angeles show and a New York show coming up, and I could go to whichever I wanted. I was traveling a ridiculous amount at that time for gigs, so the only day I could go was the New York date. I booked a flight and flew to New York with my friend Nick who choreographs and creative-directs a lot of my music videos. It was not just a concert ticket, either. They really rolled out the red carpet for us. We would get to attend sound check and hang out and sit in the VIP section.

I showed up to the Dive Bar show dressed like *Joanne*-era Lady Gaga, with the short shorts and a gray crop top. As we walked in, eyeing up all the celebrity attendees, I felt someone tap me on the shoulder and whisper in my ear, "Congratulations, you All-Star."

There she was, Lady Gaga, in high heels and sparkly blue wide-leg trouser pants. We had a brief greeting before she took the tiny stage for her sound check. Nick and I stood breathless as she went through the song "Grigio Girls" with her band just a few feet away from us. We then took our VIP seats for the Dive Bar show.

The event was sponsored by Bud Light ("just a regular girl"), which meant that's all that was on the drink menu. It was not a full concert, but instead a short set of about five songs. But by the end of the show, our table looked like a frat house because we had stacked up all these Bud Light cans and gotten quite a good beer buzz. The whole night was surreal; just getting to hear her sing in an intimate setting was incredible, but the whole VIP setup was star-studded. At one point we were sitting next to Cynthia, Lady Gaga's mom. At another point we were sitting next to Ilana Glazer and Abbi Jacobson, from *Broad City*. And still at another point we were sitting next to Robert De Niro.

Before we left, Lady Gaga invited us onto her tour bus to say hi. We went and I did a really good job of playing it cool. We talked about *Drag Race* and *All Stars* and *Joanne*. Then we took a picture and she screamed at everyone in the trailer to be quiet, because we had to do a Snapchat, saying our signature line: "We're just regular girls." It was a beautiful night. Magical.

From then on, I stayed in contact with her team. Whenever I get to see her show, she always makes it a point to invite me back to say hi afterward. She continues to create magical moments for a lot of people with her music and performances, but she really goes the extra mile to be personable and lovely. I know that people who are famous at that level do not have to be that way, but Lady Gaga doesn't just talk the talk when it comes to kindness and compassion. She also walks the walk.

That's the thing I really admire and love about Lady Gaga: how nice and kind she is to everybody, whether you're a fan or working with her. She's not about that "I'm famous, don't talk to me" bullshit. From her example, I learned a lot about how to interact with fans. I've not always succeeded in avoiding that diva attitude myself, but it's definitely something I aspire to. I thought being kind of a bitch was part of what I had to do as a famous person. The reality is, no, you don't have to do that. You can make the effort to be kind and gentle every step of the way while navigating this weird business. I especially try to encourage up-and-coming queens I meet along the way. A compliment or a word of support really does mean a lot to a young queen still trying to find her place in the world. Sometimes people think Drag queens are bitches because they require a level of resting bitch face in order to navigate a world that's out to get them. It's not easy to show up in a wig and lashes.

Lady Gaga is the genuine real deal when it comes to being a nice person, and whenever I feel ready to turn on an attitude, I think to myself, *What would Gaga do?*

THIRTY-TWO

Music

Jeremy and I had been through a lot together and somehow came out of it all with our friendship intact. Music was our bond; we always made music together, ever since I started performing. We were obsessed with the goddesses of folk music, like Stevie Nicks, Joan Baez, and Joni Mitchell. These women sang songs about the state of humanity and the state of the world. Our power as human beings. Witchy, metaphysical shit. Real shit.

All these earth mothers are directly connected to my music, though they are overshadowed by the boom-boom, electronic, dance, gay, Drag music that has become synonymous with Alaska Thunderfuck music. It's something Jeremy and I talked about constantly: How do we make a folk album without betraying our fans?

We decided to just say fuck it and dedicate an album to our folk roots. *Amethyst Journey* was born out of that. *Amethyst* because Jeremy is obsessed with stones, and *Journey* because that's really what this was. This album was going somewhere beyond where Drag music was expected to go.

For proper motivation, we went out on a retreat together, to a cabin in the woods in the Russian River Valley in Northern California. There in the wilderness we wrote together. I had come with some ideas and concepts, some voice memo recordings of possible verses. One in particular we pondered over for some time was the chorus for "So Far Gone." It's a song that came out of the misery I felt being on the road and traveling so much, away from home and my friends. After so many years of nonstop touring, I was feeling exhausted and disconnected, like a machine.

From "So Far Gone":

Will it all be gone tomorrow? You gotta strike it while it's hot
Till that dream that you've been chasing is something that it's not
Well, I still miss you, I miss my home
I miss my family, I'm so far gone

It was just like how Jeremy and I collaborated in the early days. I gave him this seedling of an idea for a song, and he extrapolated it into a beautiful composition.

We realized early on in our retreat that we were writing songs that fit into two different categories: songs about metaphysical, spiritual humanity, and songs about frivolity, getting kicked out of clubs, and getting wasted. Rather than trying to morph one category into the other, it was clear we had enough material for two separate albums, thus the creation of *Vagina*. The deep shit got to be deeper on *Amethyst Journey*, and the shallow shit got to be stupider on *Vagina*.

From "Leopard Print":

Everything must be leopard print
If it's not leopard print it's irrelevant

    Amethyst Journey didn't sell as many copies as *Vagina*. It wasn't a commercial success, but a lot of fans have expressed how much the music meant to them on a personal level, and that's been truly rewarding. But the royalty checks from *Vagina* were rewarding, too. Different kinds of rewarding, sure, but rewarding nonetheless.

THIRTY-THREE

Pod People

Willam Belli, Courtney Act, and I went to Burning Man together. Both myself and Burning Man had experienced a bit of a glow up since the first time I'd gone, though the disastrous porta potties remain. Oh my god. They are scarring.

I remember dancing with Willam and thinking about looking into that True Mirror so many years ago and realizing that even though I had nothing, I was beautiful, and I mattered. Now I had everything I'd ever dreamed of. Still, I sort of missed the grungy old days, a shitty hair piece glued to my head and mud caked under my nails.

When it was time to leave the festival, there was a line of cars building up at the exit. None of them were moving. We sat in our car for hours, at a complete standstill. Two, three, four hours went by. Nothing. Later on we found out that someone was lost and an Amber Alert had been issued. It wasn't a kidnapped child, thank Goddess. It turned out to be a teenage girl who had snuck off to get some time away from her parents, and she was totally fine. But for the rest of us, we were stuck waiting for Amber to be found.

To pass the time, we listened to a *Golden Girls* podcast called *Out on the Lanai*. The hosts, H. Alan Scott and Kerri Doherty, watched every *Golden Girls* episode, and the podcast was their subsequent discussion and dissemination of each. We ended up stuck in that car for over eight hours, and *Out on the Lanai* was our only life preserver.

As traffic cleared and our car finally began to move, Willam and I started planning out what our own podcast would be like.

"Why don't we do the same thing they are, but with *Drag Race*? We love watching it and talking shit anyway," I said.

"And we know so much about the inner workings of the show. Let's do it," Willam said.

Back in Los Angeles, we fronted some money for our experiment, since we didn't have any sponsors or anything. Then we got together with queer rapper turned producer Big Dipper, who worked with us to produce corresponding podcast episodes for the entire first season of *Drag Race*. We called it *Race Chaser*, a winking nod to the fact that many of us *Drag Race* girls had ended up sleeping with the same superfans.

Almost right away the podcast was a success. People really liked it. We teamed up with a production company, Forever Dog, and it skyrocketed from there.

Right before the COVID-19 pandemic hit, I'd planned on taking some time off. I needed to find some kind of balance in my work because I no longer had a personal life; everything was about traveling to gigs and performing. Drag was supposed to be fun; if it was becoming nothing more than a paycheck, then it would no longer be enjoyable or entertaining.

Then we were suddenly living in a pandemic. My normal avenues of work completely vanished; nonstop travel was no longer an issue. All of the *Drag Race* girls were suddenly without jobs and without income. In this new world, *Race Chaser* ended up becoming a lifesaver. Willam and I maintained a platform where we could interact with our fans even though performance venues, clubs, and bars all shut down. It's a steady job I get to apply myself to and be creative with.

Working with Willam is a dream. Our back-and-forth banter is completely natural and never forced. And because the podcast has been so successful, we had the chance to share it with our friends and sisters. Now we've added more girls into our podcast network: Latrice Royale and Manila Luzon have a podcast called *The Chop*, and Raja and Delta Work host *Very That*. These are some of the fiercest, most legendary queens of all time, in deep and funny conversations with each other.

I love getting to work with Drag queens period, but especially Ru Girls because the cleansing fires of *Drag Race* have bonded us all, whether it was a good or bad experience for us. Any time we get together, it's like kiki-ing with sisters. It's one of the things I've missed the most since the world stopped. No matter what the future brings for *Drag Race*, or for the world at large, we're all in this together.

There's something to be said for turning off and unplugging for a little bit. The pandemic was like a great big reset button, but it also reminded me of how much Drag means to me. In a lot of ways, Drag in the pandemic reminds me of what it used to be like when I first started Drag. Even my makeup has started to become more like when I first started doing Drag. I use way less glue stick now. I never liked using a glue stick; it takes too long to dry and up close it looks like shit. I would try to find ways around it. So when the pandemic started, I decided to try going without the glue stick and see how it worked out. No one noticed the difference. I actually think I look better.

Drag is such a gift to me, and it keeps unfolding and revealing itself. I'd initially started doing Drag because I thought it was cool and I gravitated toward it. Now I see it as something of cultural importance. A Drag show is a celebration of feminine power, the worship of divine feminine energy. It's almost like a religious process; we as Drag queens are the priestesses who undergo a transformation that takes no less than two hours, preferably three. When the transformation is complete, we reveal truths about our people and society.

I was worried I was going to go through a Drag burnout, but that hasn't happened. The pandemic revitalized my love of Drag. I love Drag just as much as I did when I started. It's not a job or something I feel obligated to do. There are some Drag queens who say, "Drag is a uniform I put on for work." Maybe they believe that, or maybe they say that to make it more understandable to straight people. That's not what it is for me. When I don't do Drag for an extended period of time, I feel it calling from within me, yearning to come out. Drag is an imperative. It feeds my soul, and I need it to live.

THIRTY-FOUR

I'm Going Home

It always feels good to go home.

When I'm home in Erie, Pennsylvania, everyone seems honest and straightforward, frank and funny. Maybe it's because people there still think of me as Justin. I feel like I can relax when I'm there.

My mom is in Erie; she remains my biggest fan and my constant supporter. My older sister, Brooke, lives there too, raising my niece and nephew. My nephew's so cute. He's walking and talking, and he wears glasses because he has a wandering eye. A baby with glasses? Perfection!

Los Angeles is my official home now, and I feel just as much an alien in La La Land as I did when I first moved here right out of college. Being a Drag queen in Hollywood is a surreal, strange experience, one that hasn't changed much since back then. It's the same sort of system: New girls show up in the city and work their asses off, then the next year a new round shows up. That's how the Hollywood machine works, as is displayed clearly on each new season of *Drag Race*.

I've learned how to navigate L.A. a lot better than I did back then. I was so focused on resisting and rebelling against the very idea of the Hollywood entertainment industry. Now, I sort of like it. I see it for what it is, and I can enjoy indulging in it. Jeremy lives here, and we remain close; we isolated together during the 2020 pandemic.

Like RuPaul said to Roxxxy Andrews in a rare moment of emotional sincerity, "As gay people, we get to choose our families," but historically it's been a choice made of necessity. Gays go out into the world to find a place where they belong. I found who I was in Pittsburgh, and I owe that to the family I made there. If I never went on *Drag Race*, I think I'd still be doing Drag at Blue Moon, and I'd definitely still be making music. Sharon still lives in Pittsburgh, in the same house we moved into after the fire. Veruca is still there, too, and Cherri. I don't get to see them as much as I'd like, but we all stay in touch.

As much as Sharon wanted to be an outsider, she played a major role in Drag going mainstream. She was just so good on television that the outside world swung its lookie-loo gaze right toward us and has yet to look away. Since winning *Drag Race*, she's largely pushed back against being anyone's "role model." It's a tough box she's put herself in, but she's figuring it out.

The entire ethos of Drag has changed so drastically from what it was when I started. *Drag Race* is now syndicated across the world. There was no one like me on television when I was a kid, and I watched a lot of television, so I would know. Growing up surrounded by media that doesn't see you, doesn't acknowledge you exist, can spark something inside you: a longing to be visible. Drag is the most visible expression of in-your-face queerness.

I went back to Pittsburgh recently and attended a party Sharon was hosting at Brillobox. It was a Paris Hilton–themed event. I didn't even watch the show—I was having too much fun hanging out in the back with Sharon and the other girls. In the midst of the show, there was a rumbling gasp of excitement out in the main room. Someone came in and told us what was going on: Veruca and Cherri had just walked in. Teenagers were screaming in excitement. There was going to be a House of Haunt reunion.

"Veruca's not even in . . ." Sharon started, but she stopped herself. Maturity has crept in through the cracks of her hardened veneer. Cherri and Veruca came back to the dressing room, and we had our little reunion. There was a crown on Cherri's head; she'd just won a pageant, with the assistance of Veruca.

"She just wanted you both to see she got her own crown," Veruca said.

We spent the rest of the night catching up, talking about how different everything was.

"Blue Moon's totally different now. It's all kids who grew up watching *Drag Race*," Cherri said.

"Blue Moon is where conceptual Drag goes to die," Veruca said.

For the rest of the night we gossiped like old times. Veruca was making clothes and jewelry in town, and finding success in that world. Cherri was getting back into the pageant scene, and snatching crowns apparently. We talked about her transitioning, and how it had become a hot topic in *Drag Race* and other pageant systems, many of which have antiquated rules about who they allow to do Drag. They say things like, "You can be trans but you can't have had bottom surgery," or "You can have silicone in your face but no silicone below the neck." Or "You can be trans but you have to be in the closet and present as male on a certain level to be on the show."

All these nitpicky, arbitrary restrictions are so ridiculous to me because I've always worked with so many different types of entertainers and performers. I've shared dressing rooms with every type of Drag performer, and no one has batted an eye. It's never been a question.

Drag Race had given me so much; Drag itself had given me so much. I wanted to be able to pass on the torch, which is why I started my own pageant: Drag Queen of the Year.

It started as an experiment: What if we just opened up a Drag pageant to everybody? It doesn't matter what kind of Drag you do, or how long you've been doing Drag, or how you identify or look; you can enter and you can compete.

Our first year was amazing. As the official pageant theme, leopard-print attire was highly encouraged. And that night, everything truly was leopard print. I heard from a lot of people that it was the best Drag show they'd ever seen, and I completely agree. Jackie Beat was our host, and many of my friends showed up for the judges' panel, including Gia Gunn, Peppermint, Jiggly Caliente, and Sharon Needles.

We had eight contestants, some AFAB, some nonbinary, some trans. Our final three came down to Aurora Sexton from L.A., Kat Sass from Chicago, and Abhora, who had previously appeared on *Dragula*.

For her talent, Abhora came out on stilts and performed the death drop to end all death drops. It was an honor to crown her Drag Queen of the Year.

I'm really proud of that show and can't wait to do it again. We raised a lot of money for the Los Angeles LGBT Center and showed the world how diverse Drag can be. It was the first show I did where I felt I could just enjoy the experience and get out of my own head, because it wasn't about me, it was about our contestants. There's always going to be a voice in my head telling me I could be better, could be more. Even when I became one of the most recognized Drag queens in the world, there was still that voice in my head. The key for me was to recognize that the voice is always going to be there, but that doesn't make it true. I don't have to buy into that, and it doesn't have to guide me.

Well, thank you for reading my book. I suppose I should use this final paragraph to impart some valuable piece of wisdom that will change your life. I'm hardly qualified to do that, but I'll try. Something I've learned from looking at my life story thus far is that we all have the power to take the tragic and turn it into magic. We can take those things that we hate about ourselves, or that make us feel shame, and make them into our greatest strengths. If someone calls you an ugly bitch, go out and print UGLY BITCH on a T-shirt and sell it for sixty dollars a pop. That goes for mistakes as well. When you fuck up, own it and learn from it. Maybe other people can learn from it, too. My life is still very much a work in progress, and who knows what the next chapter will hold. As the brilliant scholar Natasha Bedingfield once said, "The rest is still unwritten." And as another wise philosopher once said, "Your makeup is terrible, if you're not wearing nails, you're not doing Drag, this is my hair, you're not my read dad and you never will be, hieeee, everything must be leopard print," and most importantly, "Anus-thing is possible."

ACKNOWLEDGMENTS

Writing a book is really hard. I couldn't have done it without help.

Thank you Thomas Flannery, for helping me tell my story.

Thank you to Sharon, Veruca, Cherri, and Jeremy, for the memories.

Thank you to my management: Jacob Slane, David Charpentier, Brian Lau, and the rest of the team at Producer Entertainment Group.

Thank you to my publisher, Chronicle; my editor, Rebecca Hunt; our designer, Michael Morris.

Thank you to Magnus Hastings, for always taking the best pictures of me.

Thank you to Caldwell Linker, for always being in the wrong place at the right time.

Thank you to all the other photographers who let me use their work: Santiago Felipe, Heklina, Ves Pitts, and Jackie Beat.

PHOTO CREDITS